CHILDREN'S HEALTH

The Essential Guide

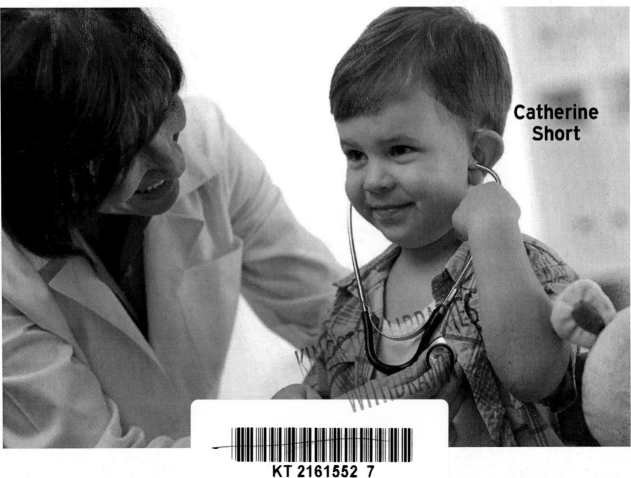

Catherine
Short

Children's Health: The Essential Guide is also available in accessible formats for people with any degree of visual impairment. The large print edition and e-book (with accessibility features enabled) are available from Need2Know. Please let us know if there are any special features you require and we will do our best to accommodate your needs.

First published in Great Britain in 2012 by
Need2Know
Remus House
Coltsfoot Drive
Peterborough
PE2 9BF
Telephone 01733 898103
Fax 01733 313524
www.need2knowbooks.co.uk

Contents

Introduction

Caring for children when they are poorly is one of the most daunting tasks for any parent, grandparent or carer. Regardless of how confident you feel normally or how much common sense you possess, I'm sure you'll agree that an ill child can send us all into blind panic. How are we to know what signs to look out for? When should we call the doctor? What does a rapidly deteriorating child look and behave like? Our instincts often tell us when danger lurks, but we don't always get it right.

The adage 'common things are common and rare things are rare' should allow us to put things into perspective, but it is often so easy to misinterpret the signs of rare and possibly life-threatening conditions. Matters become even more confusing when well-meaning friends and relatives offer unorthodox advice. And how much attention do we give to those old wives' tales that we so often hear from dear old Grandma?

Often when we telephone for help, be it for an ambulance or simply phoning NHS Direct, we unintentionally give the wrong information which could either play down the problem or inadvertently exaggerate symptoms. This could either delay urgent treatment required or cause inappropriate prioritisation of care. Wouldn't it be great if we knew with confidence, which keywords to use when phoning for help?

With this in mind, I have written this informative, easy-to-read book, packed with the most up-to-date guidance and medical evidence available, to help you to care for your child or other children in your care.

The first five chapters will focus on all the systems of the body, looking at the normal state during health and then describing how illness affects each particular body system. These chapters will also include a list of what is termed 'red flags' which are very important signs which show when a child needs urgent care and attention. Knowing what to look out for in an emergency is the key to enabling you to make timely and appropriate decisions.

Chapter 6 looks at preventing and dealing with common accidents and emergencies. Chapters 7 to 9 focus on the current childhood immunisation schedule, diet and nutrition and family travel health. Chapter 10 highlights the roles of your local doctor, health visitor, practice nurse, nurse practitioner, midwife, school nurse and pharmacist. The roles of these health professionals have evolved so much in the last five years, it is sometimes difficult to know who the most appropriate clinician is to address your needs and concerns. Here, you will find everything you need to know to help you access rapid and appropriate help.

Chapter 11 is full of helpful advice on what common treatments can be stored at home in your very own medicine chest. A full explanation on their uses will be given, including information about any common drug interactions and side effects.

You may be looking after your own children, grandchildren or working within the child social care system. Whichever is the case, by using this informative, and practical guide, you will gain the knowledge and skills to help you care with confidence.

Acknowledgements

I would like to take this opportunity to thank those of you who have given me the support and inspiration to write this book. To my husband Pete and our children Mollie and Sam, special thanks for your endless patience and encouragement.

Thank you also to Mandi Window, my photographer, and to all my colleagues at Park Road Medical Practice. Special thanks also to my good friend, and health visitor, Dianne Bridgeman, for help with chapter 6.

Disclaimer

This book is for general information about children's health and wellbeing and is not intended to replace professional medical advice.

All the information in this book was correct at the time of going to press.

The author and publishers disclaim as far as the law allows, any liability arising directly or indirectly from the use or misuse of the information found in this book.

Chapter One

Infections of the Ears, Nose and Throat

Simple anatomy and physiology

The ears belong to the auditory (hearing) system, whilst the nose and throat form part of the upper respiratory (breathing) system. When we breathe in through the nose, the air is warmed, moistened and filtered before reaching the lungs. The main respiratory structures are lined with special cells that produce mucus. This protective mucus moistens the air, trapping dust and debris. Lower down the respiratory tract, hair-like projections constantly waft any dust and debris to the mouth and throat, so that it can be expelled through coughing or swallowing. The coarse hairs lining the nose offer the same protection.

Although the mouth acts as an alternative route for air to pass, its primary function is for feeding. This will be discussed more fully in chapter 5.

The ear comprises of the external ear, the middle ear and the inner ear. Sound waves are captured and transmitted to the eardrum via the auditory canal and then received as messages of sound by the brain. The auditory canal is lined with fine hairs, sebaceous glands and glands that produce and secrete wax. The inner ear also provides the structures required for hearing and balance. The Eustachian tube provides a connection between the middle ear and the back of the throat.

'The ears belong to the auditory (hearing) system, whilst the nose and throat form part of the upper respiratory (breathing) system.'

What are the different types of infection?

The main causes of infection are of viral, bacterial and fungal origin; the most common cause being from a viral source. Let's look at the differences between viruses, bacteria and fungi.

Viral infections

Viral infections are numerous, virulent and highly contagious. Common infections of the ears, nose, throat, sinuses and chest are often caused by viruses. The same applies to flu and some diarrhoea and vomiting bugs. Normally, our own immune systems are able to fight these troublesome illnesses. However, if our immunity is low, for example during recovery from illness or at times of stress, during chemotherapy treatment or pregnancy, we can find it more difficult to recover.

'The main causes of infection are of viral, bacterial and fungal origin; the most common cause being from a viral source.'

Antibiotics do not kill viral infections. They only fight bacterial infections. Unnecessary use of antibiotics can cause side effects and drug resistance, meaning that if resistance develops, then the antibiotic may not work effectively in the future.

Sometimes, a viral infection can trigger a secondary bacterial infection which may need treating with antibiotics.

Bacterial infections

Bacterial infections are highly contagious and can affect any part of the body. Interestingly, your immune system can clear most bacterial infections without the need for antibiotics. However, antibiotics are needed if you have a serious infection such as pneumonia and meningitis. Normally, antibiotics are prescribed by a clinician although some products can be bought over the counter, such as antibiotic eye drops.

Fungal infections

Fungal infections are not easily passed from one person to another but they are very common. They thrive in warm, moist or sweaty places. Fungal infections can commonly be found in the mouth or ears, on the skin including the nails and scalp, in the groin area, under the breasts and between the legs and toes. These infections can be treated easily with antifungal creams and sometimes tablets.

Common disorders of the ears

Middle ear infection (otitis media)

This area describes the eardrum and the small space behind it. Normally filled with air, it connects to a small structure called the Eustachian tube, which links to the back of the throat. When you get a cold, the middle ear often fills up with mucus. This causes a blocked feeling and often deafness. Sometimes the mucus puts pressure on the ear drum, causing pain. Swallowing can also be painful. Sometimes this mucus becomes infected with either a virus or bacteria. Glue ear (medically known as otitis media with effusion) is a common condition that can result from persistent fluid build-up in the middle ear, where the fluid becomes thick, almost glue-like, hence the name. See overleaf for more information.

Otitis media is usually caused by a virus. Common symptoms include fever, nausea or vomiting, often with severe pain. Because it is usually caused by a virus, antibiotics are not normally recommended. Simple painkillers such as paracetamol or ibuprofen will help to alleviate the pain (see chapter 11). Encourage your child to rest and drink fluids frequently, this will reduce fever and risks of dehydration. However, if your child has earache for more than 3 days or becomes very unwell, antibiotics may be appropriate, therefore make an appointment to see your doctor or nurse practitioner. Saying this, it is reassuring to know that your immune system will normally clear the viral or bacterial infection.

Sometimes the eardrum bursts (perforates) allowing the pus to drain out, relieving the pain and the pressure behind the drum. The perforation often heals but it is important to have your child reviewed by your doctor or nurse practitioner to ensure effective healing. Also, your child should avoid getting the ears wet or going swimming until the eardrum has healed. Occasionally, the perforation will need to be corrected surgically. Also, deafness following a middle ear infection can take a few weeks to resolve once the infection has settled.

Research shows that preventative measures can be employed to protect your child from recurrent ear infections. Breastfeeding and living in a smoke-free zone reduces risk.

If your child is well but complains of earache, this may just be due to blocked Eustachian tubes. If he/she is over six years of age, they can use decongestants that can be bought over the counter or prescribed by a doctor or nurse (see chapter 11).

'Research shows that preventative measures can be employed to protect your child from recurrent ear infections. Breastfeeding and living in a smoke-free zone reduces risk.'

Glue ear

As mentioned earlier, glue ear is often due to fluid behind the eardrum or a blocked Eustachian tube. If a child suffers frequent attacks, it can lead to infection, sometimes causing chronic (long-term) hearing problems. This can often be rectified with the insertion of grommets, a tiny pipe-like structure which is inserted into the eardrum, allowing drainage. This is done through referral to an ENT (ear, nose and throat) department via your GP or nurse practitioner.

Outer ear infections (otitis externa)

Ear inflammation is usually caused by infection. Otitis externa affects the canal of the ear up to the eardrum. Normally the infection is caused by a virus or bacteria but sometimes it can be due to a fungus.

Often, otitis externa is caused by a person poking or scratching the ears with cotton buds or allowing the ear to get wet and irritated with irritants such as shampoo, soap, or even hairspray. Even using a cotton bud to clean the canal can strip the delicate lining of the skin, causing inflammation. It is just like scraping your face with sandpaper, and you wouldn't dream of doing that, would you? Otitis externa often develops in hot and humid climates. Also, it is five times more common in regular swimmers. This explains why children often return from holiday with otitis externa. Syringing ears to remove wax can also be a causative factor.

Common symptoms include itching, pain and discharge. Also hearing loss can occur and the ear can feel blocked. It can affect one or both ears simultaneously. Occasionally, the glands around your ears and neck can be affected.

Treatment for infected otitis externa is simple. Your doctor or nurse practitioner may prescribe a short course of ear drops or ear spray. These often contain a combination of antibiotic mixed with a steroid to combat inflammation and infection simultaneously. These cannot be bought over the counter at your local pharmacy. You can expect resolution of symptoms by one week. You should keep your ears dry while they are being treated. A patient information leaflet will come with your drops to show you how to use them.

You should never try and clean yours or your child(ren)'s ears yourself. Syringing should only be performed by a doctor or nurse who has experience in this procedure and you should never try it at home. Never use cotton buds either. If you get recurrent otitis externa and your doctor or nurse thinks it is due to eczema, then they will prescribe steroid ear drops which will normally be used for 1 week only.

You can help prevent recurrences by trying to keep your ears dry when swimming, showering or bathing and not using cotton buds. Also, don't use corners of towels or flannels to remove wax. You will only push the wax further into the canal.

'You should never try and clean yours or your child(ren)'s ears yourself. Never use cotton buds either.'

Trauma

This is most commonly due to the use of cotton buds which can cause inflammation and infection, but worse, can cause perforation of the eardrum, resulting in loss of hearing. Sometimes this damage cannot be repaired. Infection can also occur due to the insertion of a foreign body. This mainly affects toddlers and very young children. If you think your child has a foreign body in the ear, do not try and remove it. Go and get expert help from your GP surgery or your local minor injuries unit.

Ear wax

Wax is a naturally occurring substance which is produced and secreted by special cells in the ear canal. Surprisingly, ear wax has antimicrobial properties and secretion is a normal function, offering protection. Some people make more wax than others. Wax only becomes a problem when it causes total blockage of the canal. This prevents the sound waves transmitting to the eardrum, resulting in deafness. Syringing the ears with warm water used to be common, however, research shows that this can cause perforation. For this reason, it is performed by a specially trained clinician as a last resort.

A very effective way of reducing wax is by instilling a very small amount of warmed olive oil into each ear. Done on a daily basis for about 3 weeks, the wax should dissolve and hearing should return to normal. Wax-softening drops can be purchased from your local pharmacy. However, they are stronger than olive oil and can sometimes irritate the sensitive skin within the canal. If you are still concerned about your child's hearing, always consult your doctor or nurse practitioner as there may be another cause for hearing problems.

'Young children can expect to develop three to eight colds per year.'

Common disorders of the nose

Common cold

This is an infection caused by a virus affecting the nose and upper airways. There are many different strains of the common cold virus, which explains why they are caught so frequently. Young children can expect to develop three to eight colds per year.

Common symptoms are a blocked, runny and congested nose, often accompanied by sneezing. The discharge can be thick yellow or green and often becomes clear as things improve. Congestion often becomes worse on lying down. Also, your child will probably feel generally unwell, tired and may have a fever, a sore throat and possibly a cough. The cough is often due to mucus dripping down from the nose to the throat, which irritates the cough reflex. Generally, symptoms should settle after three or more days.

Again, for treatment of fever, sore throat and general pain, paracetamol is very effective (see chapter 11). Encourage your child to drink often. This will help liquify the secretions, prevent dehydration and soothe the throat. Sitting in a hot steamy shower room can help ease congestion too. For small babies and infants, saline drops used before feeds will help clear congestion short term and will help the child to feed.

As directed by the Medicines and Healthcare Products Regulatory Agency (MHRA) 2009, over-the-counter decongestants and cough medicines are not appropriate for children under the age of six. There has been little evidence regarding safety or effectiveness. They can also cause side effects and drug allergies.

If your child has asthma and their symptoms become worse during or following a cold, increase the use of their reliever inhaler and make an appointment to see your doctor or nurse practitioner.

Allergic rhinitis

Allergic rhinitis, or hay fever as it is more commonly known, is usually caused by an allergy to pollen. Symptoms can mimic the common cold in terms of a runny nose, congestion and itching throat. Sneezing and watery, itchy eyes can be an issue too. Surprisingly, the hay fever season begins around the beginning of February due to the early tree pollen and continues until the end of September. Normally though, sufferers will be more symptomatic during the late spring and summer months; grass pollen being the most common cause.

For those susceptible, pollens irritate the lining of the nose, causing a histamine release which in turn, causes inflammation and swelling of the soft tissues, with symptoms of itch.

Hay fever can be treated effectively with antihistamines, but if symptoms persist, nasal steroids and eye drops can be used too. These can all be purchased at your local pharmacy.

Hay fever tends to run in families, particularly if any members suffer with eczema and/or asthma. Unfortunately, hay fever can severely aggravate asthma, so again, if your child's asthma is affected, consult with your doctor or asthma nurse as soon as possible.

'Hay fever can be treated effectively with antihistamines, but if symptoms persist, nasal steroids and eye drops can be used too.'

Sinusitis

This is normally a viral infection which fills the sinus cavities of the skull with thick mucus, leading to pain, especially if the sinuses are pressed or the sufferer stoops forward. The pain can be severe, often affecting the jaw and teeth. Sinusitis is normally self-limiting, and using over-the-counter medicines such as decongestants (if over aged six) can be helpful. However, if the symptoms persist beyond ten days, the doctor will often prescribe antibiotics.

Nose bleeds

The blood vessels within the nasal septum are fragile. The most common cause of bleeding is due to nose picking, but the common cold, blowing the nose and minor injuries can also be a causative factor. Normally, the bleeding is very short-lived. Sometimes prolonged intermittent bleeding occurs due to a site of minor infection which will require treatment with antibiotic cream.

To stop bleeding:

- Encourage your child to sit up and lean slightly forward.
- Gently pinch the lower end or the bulb of the nose together for twenty minutes.
- Apply a cold compress to the face and nose to help the blood vessels to constrict.
- Do not pick or blow the nose once the bleeding has stopped. This will dislodge the newly formed scab and encourage further bleeding.
- If bleeding is heavy, get medical attention quickly. Sometimes the nose will need to be packed by a doctor to stop the flow.

Common infections of the throat

Tonsillitis

The tonsils are areas of soft glandular tissue that are not normally visible during wellness. Tonsillitis is usually caused by a virus, although sometimes it can be due to a bacterial infection. The typical symptoms of tonsillitis include a sore throat, fever, headache, nausea and tiredness with swollen glands in the neck. Your child may complain of abdominal pain and a cough. The tonsils often swell and become red. Occasionally, white patches or spots are visible lying over the tonsils. More often than not, tonsillitis is viral and it will resolve using simple painkillers. Your child should rest and even if their throat is sore, they must drink regularly, otherwise they may become dehydrated which will worsen symptoms. Paracetamol and/or ibuprofen are adequate at relieving pain, headache or fever. Gargles and throat lozenges can be effective too.

Antibiotics are not usually required to treat tonsillitis. A group of experts known as 'The Cochrane Collaboration' looked at 23 studies of proven bacterial tonsillitis and found that giving antibiotics only reduced the illness episode by 16 hours. It is reassuring to know that our immune system usually clears these infections regardless. If the infection is severe, the doctor or nurse practitioner may prescribe antibiotics, either to take immediately or in a few days if the symptoms do not settle.

'Antibiotics are not usually required to treat tonsillitis.'

Tonsils are rarely taken out these days, although your doctor will consider referring your child for surgery if he/she has had several episodes of tonsillitis in the preceding year or if bouts of tonsillitis affect school.

Quincy

Quincy, or peritonsillar abscess, is a rare complication of tonsillitis or pharyngitis, where an abscess forms next to the tonsil. It is due to a bacterial infection, normally affecting one side of the throat. Quincy is very painful. If your child really cannot swallow, not even his own saliva, he likely has a quincy and needs to attend an A&E department quickly. The quincy will need to be drained and intravenous antibiotics are required. Thankfully, a full recovery is expected.

Pharyngitis

Pharyngitis, or sore throat, is very common in children and adults of all ages. It is caused by an infection in the throat. Other symptoms may include a hoarse voice, cough, fever or headache. Your child may feel tired, sick or have swollen glands in the neck. Normally, the infection is due to a virus and should settle within a week. Pain and fever can be treated effectively with paracetamol or ibuprofen (see chapter 11).

Glandular fever (infectious mononucleosis)

'Glandular fever is known as a "self-limiting" illness, which means it normally gets better by itself.'

Glandular fever is caused by the Epstein-Barr virus. There is normally a full recovery, although it can make your child very unwell. It is known as a 'self-limiting' illness, which means it normally gets better by itself. It is commonly passed from person to person, often during kissing although it can be transmitted through sharing of cups and toothbrushes. The normal incubation period (the length of time it takes between being infected and then becoming unwell) can take up to six weeks.

The normal symptoms for glandular fever are sore throat, swollen glands, flu-like symptoms of fever, muscle aches, headaches and intense tiredness. Rarely, the spleen (a gland in the abdomen) can become swollen. The interesting thing about glandular fever is that it can mimic tonsillitis as both illnesses have pus or exudate overlying large infected tonsils. To confirm diagnosis, the doctor will send your child for a blood test.

Complications are rare, but the spleen can become swollen so it is important that your child does not do any contact sport for up to eight weeks following diagnosis. Sometimes a red rash occurs which fades quickly. Occasionally, yellowing of the skin (jaundice) can occur due to inflammation of the liver. This quickly resolves and is not serious. Often, the sufferer can feel tired and low in mood for a time following infection which can linger but should clear up in time.

There is no specific treatment for glandular fever. The best thing to do is to rest and drink plenty fluids, even if there is a sore throat. Simple painkillers such as paracetamol or ibuprofen can be taken for mild fever and pain (see chapter 11).

16

To avoid spreading the virus, your child should refrain from kissing and should avoid close body contact.

Candidal infection

This is a fungal infection affecting the mouth and tongue, most commonly as a result of prescribed antibiotic therapy. Did you know that a breastfed infant can develop symptoms if the mother has been treated with antibiotics?

Average total illness length

- Middle ear infections – 4 days.
- Colds – 1½ weeks.
- Throat infections/tonsillitis – 7 days.
- Sinus infections – 2½ weeks.

Red flags! Seek medical attention urgently for any of the following:

- A foul smelling discharge from the ear for more than ten days, this can be due to an infection called mastoiditis.
- A middle ear infection with signs of confusion which can be due to a cerebral abscess or meningitis.
- A toddler with a foul-smelling nasal discharge and a blockage on one side, as they may have obstruction due to a foreign body.
- A severe nose bleed which doesn't stop with first-aid measures, this should be dealt with at an emergency department in hospital.
- Recurrent nose bleeds.
- A child unable to swallow due to a very sore throat, leading to dribbling of saliva, you should attend A&E quickly as this is a sign of a quincy.

- A child with fever, stiff neck and/or headaches that become worse or severe with or without a rash, they could have meningitis so medical attention should be sought urgently.

- Wheezing or coughing in a known asthmatic which is not settled by their normal reliever.

- A child with persistent bleeding from the mouth – it may not be a superficial injury.

Summing Up

- Viral, bacterial and fungal infections are all associated with ear, nose and throat illnesses.

- Most infections that affect the ears and throat are due to viruses. Antibiotics have no effect on viral infections.

- Inappropriate use of antibiotics can cause 'antibiotic resistance'.

- Common ear infections include middle and outer ear infections, and glue ear.

- Wax in the ear is naturally produced by the ear canal. It offers protection against infection.

- Never clean your ears with cotton buds or the corner of your towel. If you think you have a problem, make an appointment to see your practice nurse or doctor.

- Common disorders of the nose include the common cold, hay fever and nose bleeds.

- Hay fever sometimes mimics the common cold. It can also worsen asthma symptoms.

- Tonsillitis, pharyngitis and glandular fever are common infections of the throat.

- If you or your child cannot swallow due to a sore throat, you may have an abscess called 'quincy'. Go straight to your local A&E department.

Chapter Two

Conditions Affecting the Skin and Hair

Simple anatomy and physiology

Carol Porth, (*Essentials of Pathophysiology 2004*) writes, 'The skin is one of the largest organs of the body and accounts for about 7% of total body weight in the average adult'. Isn't that amazing?

The skin provides our internal structures with protection against the environment. It is composed of three layers, the epidermis, the dermis and the subcutaneous layer. The skin also provides attachment for the hair, nails, sebaceous and sweat glands.

The outer layer, the epidermis, produces keratinocytes, cells which are essential in protecting the outer skin. Keratin is produced by the keratinocytes. These are responsible for giving the outer skin its rough texture.

The second layer, the dermis, lies between the epidermis and subcutaneous layer. The main function is to support the epidermis and to provide nutrients. A wide network of nerves is found within the dermis. The sensory pathways within the nervous system are important and allow us to recognise pain, touch, pressure and temperature changes. Blood vessels are found through all layers of the skin, providing nourishment for healthy growth and repair. The subcutaneous layer contains mainly connective tissue, providing fat stores and support and attachment to the structures within.

'The skin provides our internal structures with protection against the environment. It is composed of three layers, the epidermis, the dermis and the subcutaneous layer.'

Special cells called Langerhans cells, migrate from the bone marrow through to the epidermis and provide us with protection against invaders by activating the immune system. They are also thought to be responsible for allergic reactions in the skin.

Melanocytes produce melanin, which are the cells responsible for our skin colour. The main function of melanocytes is to provide the skin with protection against harmful ultraviolet sun rays. Exposure to the sun increases levels of melanin. This is how we become tanned.

Many of us boast a fine head of hair, but did you know that the surface of our bodies, apart from the soles, palms, genitalia and lips, is covered with fine hairs? The hair on our heads protects us from the cold and damage from the sun's rays. Eyelashes and eyebrows keep foreign bodies out of our eyes. Hair in the nose and ears protects us from invasion from bugs, dust and dirt too.

'Special cells called Langerhans cells, migrate from the bone marrow through to the epidermis and provide us with protection against invaders by activating the immune system.'

What are the common causes of injury?

Insect bites

Insect bites are common, particularly during the summer months. Common culprits are mosquitoes, midges, bedbugs and fleas. Generally speaking, the symptoms of itching and burning are mostly due to a mild allergic reaction to the bite. Often a patch of red skin will show the site of the bite, possibly with small surrounding blisters. Some blisters can become larger and may need medical attention. Often antihistamines and ice will be all that is necessary to relieve the problem. Occasionally, an insect bite can become infected and will need antibiotic treatment. See chapter 11 for more details on treatment choices.

To avoid insect bites, ask your pharmacist for a good-quality insect repellent. Also, wearing long sleeves and trousers in the mornings and during the evening can help. For information about tick bites, stings, animal and snake bites, see chapter 6.

Sunburn

Sunburn is another common cause of skin injury. Although we need to take great care to avoid sunburn, we must also remember that the summer sun's rays provide us with essential vitamin D for healthy bones and teeth. The focus here is to get a healthy balance of sun without risking sunburn. See chapter 9 for more information.

Bruises, cuts and burns

Injuries to the skin such as bruises, cuts and burns are often the result of an accident, e.g. a fall. Recommended treatment depends on the severity of the injury. See chapter 6 for more information.

What are common inflammatory skin conditions?

Acne

Acne affects teenagers of all ages but there are many treatments available. Luckily it is not contageous and will normally clear up over time. Unfortunately, it can also become infected and leave ugly scarring. At its worst, it can cause immeasurable psychological pain and despair. It can even lead to depression.

Acne is caused by a combination of factors including: hormones, poor diet, fluid retention, oil-containing cosmetics, and some drugs such as the contraceptive pill and drugs used to treat epilepsy. Normally, acne is classified as mild, moderate and severe. Mild and moderate disease can be treated with over-the-counter therapies (ask your pharmacist for advice) or by your GP or nurse practitioner but severe cases may need referral to a skin specialist called a dermatologist.

Lifestyle changes can help, such as eating a healthy diet, avoiding fizzy drinks, nuts, chocolate and coffee. Some forms of the oral contraceptive have been found to be very effective. Whichever treatment is used, it is important to encourage your teenager to persevere as most treatments take some time to become effective. Lots of encouragement and support are the key here.

Eczema

Eczema affects one in five children and can range from mild to severe. If your child is mildly affected, the main complaint can be dry skin and itching, especially when the child is warm, for example tucked up in bed or following a bath. There is no cure for eczema but it can be treated and managed successfully. Generally, most children do grow out of eczema. It can co-exist with other inflammatory or allergic conditions such as asthma and hay fever too.

'Eczema affects one in five children and can range from mild to severe.'

As well as dry, itchy, cracked skin, in more severe cases, the skin can become red and inflamed, which can sometimes lead to bacterial infections. Often the flexures, such as the wrists, ankles, neck and behind the knees, can be affected. As the skin's integrity is impaired when it is broken, opportunistic infections such as impetigo can become a secondary infection.

How can I treat my child's eczema?

To reduce the distressing effects of eczema, you need to keep your child's skin soft and well hydrated by regularly using an emollient such as E45 cream, Doublebase Gel or Hydromol. If your child's main complaint is the itch, you can use Eurax cream to treat this. See chapter 11 for more details.

For red, inflamed skin, a mild steroid cream may be all that is necessary. Mild steroid creams can be purchased at your pharmacy, but if the inflammation is severe, you should consult with your nurse practitioner or GP. A more potent steroid may be necessary. In general, steroid creams for short-term use are safe and effective. One week of use should solve the problem. If not and you are tempted to use the cream for longer, seek medical advice as an alternative may be necessary.

To help reduce symptoms of eczema:

- Avoid using soap, as this dries out the skin. You can get a soap substitute from your pharmacy or surgery which will not aggravate the skin.

- Wash all clothing in non-biological soap powder. Do not use fabric softener either. Pollens attach themselves to clothing when drying them on a washing line, so if your child has pollen allergy this may worsen their eczema. If you suspect this may be a cause, try drying the clothes in a dryer or in the house.

- Antihistamines can be effective in the short term. See chapter 11 for details.

As a further point of reference, see *Eczema: The Essential Guide* (Need2Know).

Heat rash

Heat rash commonly affects babies and small children. Simply by removing them from the heat, such as moving them into the shade or a cool area, can help. Removing clothing will also help. You can use calamine lotion to sooth the skin. See chapter 11 for details.

Hives

Hives, or urticaria, produce itching red wheals that resemble nettle rash. Often hives can occur for no particular reason. Sometimes it is the result of an allergic reaction or extremes of temperature as in episodes of fever. Very often a cause cannot be found. You can treat hives effectively with antihistamines if you feel the reaction is allergic in nature. If your child has a fever, reduce clothing and give baby or children's calpol. If the condition doesn't settle or your child is unwell, you should contact your surgery for an appointment.

Nappy rash

Nappy rash is commonly found around the nappy area. Most babies are affected at one time or another and it is caused by the skin coming into prolonged contact with urine and stool (poo).

'Often hives can occur for no particular reason. Sometimes it is the result of an allergic reaction or extremes of temperature as in episodes of fever.'

To prevent nappy rash:

- Change your baby's nappy regularly, especially if they have just soiled it.

- Disposable wipes can irritate so switch to warm water for cleaning your baby's bottom. Ensure you dry properly by patting rather than rubbing the skin.

- Allow your baby to lie on a baby mat without a nappy on for a few minutes. Babies love this too.

- Avoid using talcum powder.

If your child gets nappy rash, you can easily treat this with an effective barrier cream such as Morhulin ointment or Drapolene cream. See chapter 11 for more details.

If the rash becomes worse, speak to your pharmacist or book an appointment at your surgery. The rash may be developing a secondary bacterial infection and may require antibiotic cream.

What are common bacterial skin conditions?

Impetigo

Impetigo is a bacterial skin infection usually caused by a bacterium called staphylococcus aureus. It can affect either healthy skin or cracked, broken skin such as eczema. You may notice small watery blisters first which then burst and become scabby. They can sometimes look like golden crusts. This infection is most commonly seen on the face, particularly around the nose and mouth. It is very contagious and is most often seen in children.

How can I treat impetigo?

- A severe infection can sometimes occur, it is important to treat quickly. Your doctor or practice nurse will prescribe either antibiotic cream or medicine. You cannot buy this over the counter.

- Clean the crusts off with warm soapy water before applying the cream. Pat dry and do not share towels to prevent spreading to others. Also do not share flannels or bath water.

- Wash your hands thoroughly after cleaning your child or applying antibiotic cream.

- Discourage your child from touching the scabs or lesions.

- If the infection is spreading or your child becomes unwell, consult your doctor or nurse practitioner urgently.

- Exclude your child from the childminder, nursery or school until the crusting has gone.

What are common viral skin conditions?

Chickenpox

Chickenpox is a common childhood illness which causes a red, small, patchy rash which quickly develops into small water blisters. The blisters quickly burst and then dry up. If your child has chickenpox, they are contagious until the last scab dries up – usually by day seven. The disease is spread through droplet infection when the blisters burst and those who have never had the disease may be infected. Once infected, it can take between seven and twenty-one days to become ill.

Normally a child will only be slightly unwell with chickenpox. If they have a high fever or are very unwell, particularly if they have a cough, they need to be seen by a nurse practitioner or doctor. In rare cases, pneumonia can occur in high-risk children.

There is no vaccine available as yet within the UK childhood immunisation programme. However this may change.

You can treat the symptoms of itching and discomfort with antihistamines. Offer baby or children's paracetamol if your child becomes unwell. Keep your child's fingernails short to help reduce injury to the skin through scratching.

'If your child has chickenpox, they are contagious until the last scab dries up – usually by day seven.'

Cold sores

Cold sores are caused by the herpes simplex virus. The infection starts with tingling, itching or burning to the lips, followed by development of small watery blisters. They are highly contagious and pass from person to person through contact during the blistering phase. Left alone, they will usually resolve after seven to ten days. Alternatively, you can buy antiviral cream from your pharmacy which, used as soon as the tingling starts, will speed up the healing process.

Remember, your child can pass this on so he or she should use their own towels and avoid contact with others until the blisters have all dried up. It is important that they stay away from any newborn babies or anyone who is on chemotherapy, or who is known to have HIV.

'If your baby develops cradle cap, rub the scalp with warm olive oil.'

Cradle cap

Cradle cap or infant seborrhoeic dermatitis produces white and yellow waxy scales which can be seen on the scalp. Although it can look unsightly, do not be alarmed. The condition is entirely harmless and will often clear up after a few weeks without requiring treatment. Young babies are often affected but it can affect older children too.

To prevent cradle cap wash your baby's head regularly. If your baby develops cradle cap, rub the scalp with warm olive oil. Leave for a while to soak into the scales then brush the affected area with a baby brush. This will help to loosen the scales. Follow this by shampooing the scalp.

Warts and verrucas

Warts and verrucas are commonly found on the hands and feet and are caused by human papillomavirus (there are over 100 known strains of HPV). They are very common and are spread from person to person, often at the swimming baths. Those with eczema can be more at risk. Although harmless, they can be painful, especially when they are on the feet, due to pressure on shoes and during walking.

You can leave them alone and they can disappear, although this may take up to two years.

To treat warts you can:

- Use salicylic acid preparations purchased at your local chemist.

- Apply duct tape – no kidding – see the box below for details.

- See your practice nurse or doctor to have them frozen with liquid nitrogen.

To treat a wart with duct tape:

1. Wash the area and dry completely.

2. Apply duct tape and leave for a week.

3. Remove the duct tape then wash and dry the area. Rub with an emery board and leave without treatment overnight.

4. Clean and dry the area and reapply the duct tape for a further week and then repeat until the wart has gone.

'Headlice are not fussy. They like either clean or dirty hair.'

What are common parasitic infections?

Headlice

Headlice and nits are parasites which do not cause illness but they are a nuisance. Most children will come into contact with headlice through close contact with others who are currently infested. Headlice are not fussy. They like either clean or dirty hair. They are flesh coloured and live on infected hair, close to the scalp. The eggs are dark and hard to see. Once the egg has hatched, the eggs turn white and are more visible. The empty eggs are then known as nits. If you suspect your child has headlice, you need to investigate thoroughly.

How to check for headlice:

- Wash your child's hair as normal and towel dry.

- Comb your child's hair smooth using plenty of conditioner. Do not rinse off the conditioner.

- Using a nit detection comb, which can be purchased from your local chemist, comb from the roots at the scalp to the tips of the hair, ensuring that every part of the scalp is combed thoroughly. Pay particular attention to the nape of the neck and behind the ears.

- Keep checking the comb for lice.

- If you find living lice, everyone in the family needs checking.

- If you find living lice, go to your local pharmacy for insecticide treatment.

To prevent further infection and passing it on:

- Check regularly and treat if needed.

- Tell your child not to share combs or hair brushes.

- Inform your child's nursery or school if you have found living lice.

- Tell close contacts to check their own and their child(ren)'s hair. This will help to break the cycle of re-infestation.

Scabies

Scabies is a skin condition caused by a parasite or mite, which tunnels under the layers of the skin and deposits their eggs within the burrow. The lavae then hatch, creating their own burrow. It takes ten to fifteen days for an egg to develop to an adult. The adult mites live for about four to six weeks. It can take some time before the itch associated with scabies occurs. The itch is a result of infection. The itchy rash caused by the mite can be found between the fingers, thighs, under the armpits, around the bottom and genitals. Often, you can see wavy silver or grey lines of burrows, and if you look carefully, you may see a mite at the end of the line or burrow.

Scabies is more common in children and young adults, especially in urban areas. It is also more common in winter. It is mainly transmitted through direct contact, although it can be transmitted through clothing, bedding and furniture.

You should book an appointment at your surgery if you suspect scabies. Do not be alarmed as scabies can be treated easily with permethrin 5% dermal cream or malathion 0.5% aqueous liquid. You can get this on prescription. To stop the infection, all members of the household and close contacts should be treated at the same time, on the same day, to reduce the chance of re-infection. Remember also to machine wash all bedding, clothes and towels at fifty degrees Celsius to also prevent re-infestation.

Red flags! Seek medical attention urgently for any of the following:

- Any rash that develops as a result of a new medicine.

- A dark red or purple bruise-like rash that doesn't blanch when pressed with a glass.

- A burn which is larger than the size of the victim's palm.

- A wound that doesn't stop bleeding or is deep.

Summing Up

- The skin is the largest organ of the body and it protects the internal structures from infection and injury.

- Common causes of injury to the skin include, bites and stings, sunburn, cuts and burns.

- Common inflammatory conditions include acne, eczema, heat rash and nappy rash.

- Infections of the skin can include impetigo, chickenpox, cold sores, cradle cap, warts and verrucas.

- Headlice can live on clean or dirty hair. They are hard to see with the naked eye.

- Parasitic infestations can affect the whole family. Re-infestation can be prevented by regular checking.

- A rash which is a result of a new medication needs urgent medical attention.

Chapter Three

Common Chest and Breathing Problems

Simple anatomy and physiology

The respiratory system consists of the nose, mouth, throat (pharynx) voice box (larynx), windpipe (trachea), airway tubes (bronchi and bronchioles) and two soft, spongy lungs. The lungs and the main airways are found in the chest cavity, along with the heart and great blood vessels and the gullet (oesophagus). All these structures are protected by the ribcage and the breastbone.

The respiratory system provides our bodies with a means to exchange vital gases, those being oxygen and carbon dioxide. Oxygen from the air is inhaled and transported around the body through the blood system and carbon dioxide is eliminated in the same way. The air that we breathe is warmed and filtered through the nose, throat and windpipe. Fluid from the membranes lining these structures moistens the air. Mucus from special 'goblet cells' within these structures provide protection by entrapping foreign particles and dust which are then wafted upwards by special hair-like structures called cilia, which move constantly, pushing the waste products up towards the throat, just like an internal cleansing system. This is then coughed up or swallowed.

The function of coughing helps to prevent the accumulation of secretions and dust from entering the lung tissue, therefore the cough reflex is vital in providing us with protection. Saying that, frequent and prolonged coughing can cause pain, exhaustion and in some cases, especially in children, it can cause undesirable effects of the elastic tissues on the lungs, and on the heart.

What are the most common types of infection?

As mentioned in more detail within chapter 1, the most common types of infection are caused by viruses and bacteria; the most common cause coming from a viral source. Generally, all infections can be transmitted, either through person-to-person contact, via airborne sources or from inanimate objects such as touching dirty toys, door handles, loo seats and the like. Programmed to fight infection, our immune systems generally do a great job. For most of us, infections are a mild concern. Unfortunately, they can be much worse for others, particularly in those with immune suppression for whatever reason. Also, the elderly and the very young can be more at risk.

What are common chest conditions and what care is needed?

Asthma

Asthma is an inflammatory disease prevalent in all age groups, particularly children, which affects the airways. In-between episodes, your child may have no breathing problems. Asthma occurs due to exposure to a trigger. A trigger is anything that causes inflammation within the airways which can lead to wheezing, coughing and shortness of breath. Common triggers include, the house dust mite, animal dander, pollen, aerosols, perfumes, extremes of temperature, emotion, exercise, some medicines such as ibuprofen or Nurofen, and moulds. Some foodstuffs have also been identified.

Asthma symptoms can become more troublesome when an asthmatic is suffering with the common cold or flu. Other upper respiratory infections such as tonsillitis can exacerbate asthma too.

Small babies and children are more susceptible to developing asthma if there is a family history of asthma, hay fever or eczema, particularly from the maternal side of the family. It is difficult for a doctor or nurse to diagnose asthma in babies and children under eight as they are not able to perform special lung function tests which help confirm the condition. Diagnosis is made on listening to the parents carefully regarding the child's symptoms.

'Asthma occurs due to exposure to a trigger. A trigger is anything that causes inflammation within the airways which can lead to wheezing, coughing and shortness of breath.'

If asthma is suspected, under careful guidance of a specially trained clinician, your child will be started on a trial of treatment designed to reduce asthmatic symptoms. Usually, this treatment is called a bronchodilator; a gas propelled medicine which is usually given through an inhaler with a tube-like structure called a spacer attached to a face mask. You should give this medicine when your baby or child is troubled by a cough, wheeze or shortness of breath. It is important that you monitor the response to the inhaler and advise your doctor or nurse when your child attends for review. There are a variety of medicines used in asthma and your clinician will choose the best one to control your child's symptoms, depending on the severity of the symptoms.

To reduce asthma symptoms:

- Try and avoid any known triggers, especially cigarette smoke. Some triggers are unavoidable, such as pollens, but you can reduce exposure by shutting the window at night and taking an antihistamine to reduce the allergic response. Replacing carpeting with laminate flooring is helpful, as is the use of a dehumidifier.

- Damp dust the home regularly if this is a trigger. Also use hypoallergenic pillows and duvets and wash bedclothes at sixty degrees.

- Put all soft toys into plastic bags and then into the freezer regularly to kill house dust mites. Defrost and vacuum before giving back to your child.

- Avoid extremes of temperature.

- Ensuring your child is immunised against influenza will offer protection. See chapter 7, where childhood immunisations will be explained in more detail.

- If your child needs to use their reliever inhaler more than three times per week or is waking during the night because of their asthma, it is time to book an appointment at your surgery for an asthma check.

'In an asthma attack, the muscles of the air passages in the lungs go into spasm. As a result, the airways become narrowed, which makes breathing difficult'. *The First Aid Manual – Revised 9th Edition, (2011)*.

For more information about asthma including how to recognise and manage an attack, visit www.asthma.org.uk. Also, see *Asthma: The Essential Guide*, (Need2Know).

Bronchiolitis

Bronchiolitis is usually due to a viral infection within the bronchioles of the lower respiratory system, the lungs, causing swelling and obstruction of the smaller airways. It is one of the most common causes of hospitalisation where there are 20,000 admissions each year. Currently in Britain, 3% of infants are admitted due to this infection but the numbers are rising, possibly due to the increased survival rate of premature infants.

Usually affecting children under the age of one, this infection occurs in epidemics, most often in the winter months. Incidents increase combined with certain risk factors such as passive smoking, overcrowding and infection from older siblings and nursery children. It has been suggested that breastfeeding has a protective effect. The disease appears to be more severe in those of low birth weight, premature birth, under the age of three months, in the presence of other respiratory diseases such as cystic fibrosis, heart problems, those who may be immunosuppressed and those with Down's Syndrome.

The symptoms are similar to those of the common cold, including an irritable cough, runny nose, rapid breathing, mild fever and poor feeding. Some children may wheeze or vomit. Your child may have a mild infection, where dosing with their normal dose of Calpol, rest and plenty of fluids, may allow resolution. However, if any signs of respiratory distress are seen, call for an ambulance.

Signs of respiratory distress:

* Rapid breathing with leaning forward and possible dribbling.

* Stopping breathing for longer than ten seconds.

* Flaring nostrils or grunting.

* Pulling the chest in at the ribs, below the breastbone or above the collarbone.

* Blue colour to baby or child's skin.

Influenza (flu)

Influenza is a viral infection which affects the lower respiratory tract. There are three main types, A, B and C. Influenza A and B cause most infections.

Infection rates increase mainly during the winter, between the months of December and March. Did you know that up to 15% of the population can develop flu in any one year? Flu is a nasty, debilitating illness but it can be dangerous in certain 'at risk groups' such as diabetics; asthmatics; those with kidney or liver disease and those immunosuppressed for example, those on steroids; those with HIV; those on cancer treatment; the very old and the very young. In 1918, the Spanish flu reached pandemic proportions, which killed 21 million worldwide. Remember swine flu which caused a massive immunisation programme in 2009?

Flu is transmitted through droplet infection, when those with the infection cough or sneeze. They may also pass germs by touching shared things such as door handles, with infected hands. It is really important to remind children and adults to wash and dry hands thoroughly, especially after coughing or sneezing. After being infected, you can develop the infection for a couple of days before the symptoms present. This is called the incubation period.

The common symptoms of flu are:

- Appetite loss, feeling sick and poor feeding in small babies and infants.
- General weakness or lethargy.
- Headache and painful muscles and joints.
- Fever – very small children may have a convulsion or 'fit' due to a high fever.
- Dry cough with possibly a sore throat.

Some may develop an upset stomach but this is not usual. A runny nose with sneezing is usually due to the common cold and is not normally seen in flu. The collection of symptoms usually improve over a number of days, although the cough and weakness may last for one to two weeks. Your child is still infectious for up to five days after the start of symptoms. Some will remain infectious for up to two weeks and those who are immunosuppressed can still spread the disease for weeks.

How do I care for my child with flu?

Normally, resting at home, drinking plenty of fluids to prevent dehydration and a calming restful environment is all that is required. Calpol or ibuprofen for pain and fever will help. Staying at home will prevent passing on the infection.

Over-the-counter cough and cold remedies are not available for children under the age of six. There is no evidence that they work and side effects have been known.

'Over-the-counter cough and cold remedies are not available for children under the age of six. There is no evidence that they work and side effects have been known.'

In severe cases, your doctor may prescribe antiviral tablets which stop the multiplication of the virus. They have been found to reduce complications in those deemed higher at risk. Antiviral medicine is only normally used when there is an epidemic or pandemic or if the child is especially at risk or unwell. As flu is a viral illness, antibiotics are not usually prescribed. However, if your child develops a secondary bacterial infection, then antibiotics may be prescribed.

Complications are rare but can affect those groups of people with other illnesses such as diabetes, asthma and other chest problems. Acute bronchitis is a common complication. Sometimes the child can develop secondary pneumonia. See the 'red flags' section in this chapter for more information.

How can I protect my child?

If your child falls into one of the 'at risk groups' as shown in the below list, they are entitled to the influenza injection. It is very important that your child is offered this vaccine, as it will protect him/her and prevent development of secondary disease. For more detail, see chapter 7 'Childhood Immunisations Explained'.

At risk groups for influenza include:

- People aged over 65.

- Sufferers of long-term lung diseases such as asthma and cystic fibrosis.

- Any child who has previously been hospitalised due to a chest infection.

- People with heart, kidney or liver disease.

- Diabetics
- People with poor immunity.
- Previous stroke patients (although rare, babies can have these) and neurological disorders such as multiple sclerosis.
- Those who work as a carer, nurses, doctors, care home staff, carer for the elderly or chronically ill.

NB If your child does not fall into any of the above at risk groups, a flu jab is not necessary. He/she is not at risk of developing complications as a result of flu.

Pneumonia

Pneumonia is a serious infection of the lungs. Treatment normally requires antibiotics. Most people will recover fully, however it may be life-threatening. This respiratory infection can be caused by either a virus or bacteria. Sometimes fungi and yeasts can be the causative factor. Although rare, gastric secretions can be inhaled and cause 'aspirational pneumonia'. Once infected, the germs quickly spread down the airways causing inflammation and excessive fluid production which fills up the air pockets (alveoli), preventing exchange of gases.

What are the symptoms of pneumonia?

- Worsening cough and sputum production which is sometimes bloodstained.
- Breathing fast or becoming breathless.
- Appetite loss and sometimes stomach pain.
- Fever and sweats.
- Headaches, aches and pains, also sharp pain in the chest.

The above symptoms mimic those of influenza. If concerned, call your doctor or if signs of respiratory distress are seen, call an ambulance.

Can pneumonia be prevented?

Since the introduction of the pneumococcal vaccine, infection rates have declined. See chapter 7 for more details about immunisation.

Also, cigarette smoke can severely affect a child's health, including, asthma, pneumonia, otitis media and wheezing. Cigarette smoke has also been found to increase the risk of cot death.

If you would like help in stopping smoking, visit your practice nurse or pharmacist, where you can get expert advice. Also see *Stop Smoking: The Essential Guide* (Need2Know).

How do I care for my child with pneumonia?

Babies and children would normally be cared for in hospital under close supervision and be allowed home once the child is stable. Antibiotics are prescribed which usually work well. Once home, the usual advice would be to keep warm, drink plenty of fluids to prevent dehydration, eat when hungry and rest. Normal eating patterns will return when your child improves.

Inhalation of a foreign body

A rapid onset of whistling or a wheezing sound heard on breathing in a child not known to be ill could be a sign that he or she has inhaled a foreign body, causing it to lodge in the windpipe or trachea. This is more common in small children and toddlers. The child may appear calm. On the other hand, inhaling a larger foreign body, such as a small coin or marble, will probably cause the child to wheeze, cough and be distressed. They may also have a bluish tinge to the nose, ears and lips. This is called cyanosis and is always a medical emergency. Seek medical advice urgently. Always protect small children by only allowing them to play with age-appropriate toys.

Whooping cough

Whooping cough is caused by a severe infection in the upper airways. It is usually more severe in infants under the age of three months. However, in older children and adults, the symptoms are milder. This disease can be fatal in young children, which is why immunisation against this and other infectious diseases is very important. Again, please visit chapter 7 for more details.

The illness first presents with signs of a common cold, for example a runny nose, catarrh, sneezing and a high fever. After one or two weeks, the initial symptoms fade, replaced by a hacking cough, where the child may cough and cough repeatedly, almost as if the lungs are being emptied, before finally drawing in breath. This may be followed by the characteristic 'whoop'. The child may also make a gasping or choking sound and flail their arms and legs about, the eyes may bulge and water and the face may go red. This truly distressing cough may cause vomiting, often leaving the child exhausted.

Around 50% of children are admitted to hospital, where the child will usually be treated with antibiotics and those in contact with the child may be offered 'prophylactic' treatment of antibiotics to prevent spread.

The cough may persist for up to three months, which is why it used to be called 'the 100 days cough'. Interestingly, older children and adults may not whoop at the end of the coughing spasm. If you suspect your child is suffering with whooping cough, you must seek urgent medical attention.

'Croup is usually caused by a number of viral infections which are more prevalent during the autumn and winter months.'

Croup

Croup is usually caused by a number of viral infections which are more prevalent during the autumn and winter months. It affects the upper airways, causing swelling and thick mucus around the larynx (voice box) and trachea (windpipe). There is some evidence to suggest that recurrent croup may be due to an allergic factor. Croup mostly affects children under the age of four, but may affect older children, adolescents and adults. Your child may start with a simple runny nose, sore throat and a mild fever, which leads to a barking cough which is usually worse at night. Parents often liken the sound of the cough to the sound that a seal makes when barking. You may also notice your child wheeze when breathing in. This is called 'stridor'. The illness tends to last between three and seven days but sometimes can continue for up to two weeks. Be reassured that complications are rare and less than 5% of children require hospital admission.

Most cases of croup are mild and can be managed at home. Antibiotics are not an effective treatment as the infection is due to a virus. However, a doctor may prescribe these if he suspects that your child has another secondary infection which could be bacterial. Your doctor may prescribe a single oral dose of steroid therapy. This has been found to be effective. Also, rest and a calm atmosphere will help, as crying and upset causes strain on the already compromised lung function. Give paracetamol and ibuprofen to control fever and pain. It is also important to ensure your child is drinking plenty to avoid dehydration. Your child needs to eat healthy, nutritious food when ill, so anything like home-made soup, fruit smoothies and small healthy snacks and meals will help.

I have found that steam treatment is a very effective way to ease this type of cough. If you have a shower, put the shower on full heat, with doors and windows closed and when the bathroom is lovely and full of steam, sit in the bathroom with your child and play or read a book until their breathing settles. This can take about twenty minutes. Obviously, take great care that your child is safe from scalding. If your child doesn't improve, especially if they show any signs of respiratory distress, call for an ambulance.

Tuberculosis (TB)

Although this infection used to be less prevalent, more recently, cases have risen. More worryingly, 10% of cases have become antibiotic-resistant. Prevention is through immunisation. For information on childhood immunisations see chapter 7.

Tuberculosis is transmitted through droplet infection, meaning that the mycobacterium, which can survive for long periods of time, has been inhaled from infected air. A lesion or scar forms within the lung tissue. In the early stages of the disease, there may be no symptoms but the lesions can spread and then become detected in sputum, where it can spread again through droplet infection.

What are the symptoms of TB?

In more advanced disease, the symptoms include low-grade fevers, night sweats, extreme tiredness, failure to thrive, weight loss, loss of appetite and a cough which starts as a dry cough, later becoming more productive with possible streaks of blood. Also breathlessness can be a feature. A chest X-ray and sputum sample will be obtained from anyone suspected of contracting TB. Contact tracing is performed on close contacts. This is done in the form of a Mantoux test; a blood test which diagnoses latent TB in contacts.

Management of TB

This disease is a notifiable disease, in that it will be reported to the local public health department to assist with surveillance data and to initiate contact tracing. The doctor is responsible for notifying this disease. Suspected cases will be admitted to hospital and are usually nursed in a separate side ward until they are non-infectious.

Red flags! Seek medical attention urgently for any of the following:

- Cyanosis (blue lips, tips of ears, finger or toenails) with or without drowsiness or lethargy.

- Low-pitched stridor, with very sore throat, high fever, difficulty in swallowing, and signs of respiratory distress means the child may be suffering with epiglottitis.

- Nostril flaring, leaning forward, panting, dribbling, drooling, these are signs of respiratory distress.

- Suspicion of an inhaled foreign body with or without wheezing.

- Sudden or worsening shortness of breath and/or confusion.

- Shortness of breath following a sports injury or minor injury to the chest.

- Persistent cough following travel abroad, particularly to the Indian sub continent, this could be tuberculosis.

- Severe shortness of breath for no reason, with facial swelling, pale skin and itching, this may be a sign of severe allergic reaction – if you can, administer antihistamine while awaiting an ambulance.

- Dry skin, dry mouth and dry lips, these are signs of dehydration.

- Coughing up blood, this always needs urgent medical attention.

Summing Up

- The respiratory system provides us with a means to exchange vital gases, oxygen and carbon dioxide, to maintain life.

- Infections affecting the respiratory system are either viral or bacterial including influenza, bronchiolitis, pneumonia, whooping cough, croup and tuberculosis.

- Asthma is common in children and can be caused by a variety of triggers, including dust and pollens, animal dander, viruses, bacteria and moulds, exercise and allergies.

- Bronchiolitis, flu, whooping cough and croup are some of the most common childhood chest complaints.

- Cyanosis, nostril flaring, grunting and stridor are all signs of a medical emergency – call 999.

- Many childhood illnesses can be prevented through effective immunisation. Ensure your child has had all their jabs.

Chapter Four

Conditions Affecting the Eyes

Simple anatomy and physiology

The spherical-shaped eyeball is mobile and fits within a pyramid-shaped cavity, commonly known as the orbit of the skull. There are three layers to the eye: a fibrous layer, a vascular layer and the retina where the nerve supply is found. The eyeball is filled with fluid which aids penetration of light toward the retina at the back of the eye. The eyelids protect the exposed areas of the eyeball. The underside of both the upper and lower lids and the eyeball are covered by a thin, clear mucus layer, called the conjunctiva. Visual information is transmitted from the retinal cells to the brain via the optic nerve.

What are the common causes of infection and injury?

Following are a number of common eye conditions that affect people of all ages. Differing conditions can look similar to the untrained eye, so it is important that you seek advice if you suspect an eye infection. If your pharmacist is unable to offer advice, you will need to make an appointment with your doctor or nurse practitioner.

Conjunctivitis

Conjunctivitis, or red eye, is one of the most common disorders of the eyes in all age groups, particularly children. This condition causes the eye to become red and inflamed. The eye can feel gritty and uncomfortable. Conjunctivitis can be caused by a virus, bacteria, chlamydia, or an allergy. The treatment and management is different for each.

- Bacterial conjunctivitis normally starts in one eye first and can spread to the other. There is profuse sticky yellow or green discharge from the eye and it can be difficult to open, especially in the morning. Very often, the condition has been spread from another person.

> 'Conjunctivitis,,or red eye, is one of the most common disorders of the eyes in all age groups, particularly children.'

Chloramphenicol eye drops are an effective treatment which can be prescribed by your doctor or nurse practitioner. These are used four times per day, for a week. You can bathe the child's eyes with cooled boiled water on cotton wool. Remember it is a contagious condition which means that your child cannot attend school or nursery until the symptoms have subsided. They will need to use a separate towel and stay away from anyone who is immunosuppressed, for example, undergoing chemotherapy or pregnant.

- Viral conjunctivitis often occurs at the same time as a viral upper respiratory infection. Both eyes may be equally affected, feel gritty and sore and be red in appearance. The discharge is normally watery and can go on for many weeks. Often, this viral infection will settle without treatment,. However, chloramphenicol eye drops offer relief and prevent secondary bacterial infections.

- Chlamydia conjunctivitis often affects the very young with green or yellow mucus discharge from both eyes. Newborn infants can contract this during birth. For this reason, it is very important for any baby under the age of one month to be examined by a doctor. Even if the infection is not chlamydia, infection in the very young can cause corneal disease and blindness.

- Allergic conjunctivitis can occur at any time of the year but is more prevalent in the spring and summer and is associated with hay fever. The most common complaint is itching and red eye. The discharge is clear and stringy. Allergic eye drops such as Opticrom eye drops can be used for children and adults for symptomatic relief. Also, antihistamine tablets or oral medicine from your pharmacy can be used simultaneously.

Blepharitis

Blepharitis is a very common condition, affecting all ages. Those affected are often bothered by persistently sore, gritty eyes and eyelids. The edges around the eyes become inflamed with crusts around the eyelashes. Conjunctivitis can be present concurrently. As blepharitis is known to be a chronic disease, the focus is to manage the condition and prevent secondary infections. Gently clean around the lid margins with a cotton bud, soaked in baby shampoo and water. This helps remove the fatty lipid crusts and prevents infection. Antibiotic eye ointment may be prescribed to treat bacterial infection. Also, artificial tears may be of benefit and provide relief of symptoms of dry eye, which is also associated with blepharitis.

Blunt injury

Any eye injury, large or small must be reviewed by an eye unit. The smaller the object, the more damage can be caused. A large object can forcibly damage the protective bony structures around the eye and a smaller object can cause damage to the structures of the eye. It is important to seek medical attention fast, as damage may not be initially obvious. If there is blurring of vision, this tells you that medical attention is required urgently. The advice is the same in the presence of any bleeding, dislike of light, double vision, sluggish eye movements or eye injury with nose bleed.

Penetrating injuries and cuts

These all need specialist attention. Any laceration around the eye will need stitching. Sometimes there are not obvious signs of a penetrating injury, but if you suspect this, do not delay seeking advice. Penetrating wounds can be a result of injury with a hammer and chisel, glass, thorns, knives, darts and pencils, for example.

Orbital cellulitis

This condition can cause blindness and is potentially life-threatening. This dangerous infection often begins from infected sinuses. If children are not treated quickly, it can result in blindness within a few hours. Signs of this rare but dangerous infection usually include a very swollen eye lid, with limited eye movement and tenderness on pressing under the cheekbones and under the eyebrows, i.e. over the sinuses. If you suspect this condition, attend your local eye hospital or A&E department without delay.

Chalazion

'Squints are common in children where there is a family history. A constant squint has a worse prognosis that one that is intermittent.'

These lumps are due to an overgrowth of tissue called a granuloma, which lies underneath the lid, causing swelling and pain. It can be a result of a blocked duct. The lump can be hard and inflamed. It also can cause blurring of vision. This can be treated with antibiotic ointment. Bathing with a warmed flannel can help too. A small surgical procedure under a local anaesthetic may be necessary.

Styes

These are commonly confused with chalazion. A stye is caused by an infection of the eyelash follicle. It causes a tender, inflamed lump at the lid margin. Unlike a chalazion, a head of pus may develop which can be treated with a warm compress to help discharge of the pus. Antibiotic ointment treats the bacterial infection.

Squint

Squints are common in children where there is a family history. A constant squint has a worse prognosis that one that is intermittent. The earlier the onset, the more likely the child will require surgery. If you suspect a squint, always seek advice from your doctor.

Need2Know

Red flags! Seek medical attention urgently for any of the following:

* Eye pain, blurred vision or loss of vision, attend your local eye hospital or accident and emergency unit immediately.

* Severe sudden swelling to one or both eyes where the crease to the upper lid balloons out, and/or limited eye movement and/or tender sinuses; this requires immediate medical attention as this could cause blindness.

* If you suspect that a foreign body, such as a stick, piece of glass or twig has scratched an eye, this also needs urgent attention. The eyeball needs to be stained with a fluorescent eye drop and examined with specialist equipment.

* If your infant is under the age of four weeks and develops a red eye, take the child to your nearest A&E department.

* If your child develops chickenpox blisters in or around the eyes make sure you visit your GP to have check-up.

* Flashing lights or floaters, these are always serious and demand medical treatment.

Summing Up

■ Eye infections are common in children and are usually caused by viruses and bacterial infections.

■ A baby under the age of four weeks with an eye infection needs urgent medical attention.

■ In minor infections, bathe the eyes with cooled boiled water to relieve discharge and symptoms of itch.

■ If your child has an eye infection, ensure they use their own towel and flannel, otherwise the infection can spread.

■ Do not send your child to school or nursery if they have an eye infection.

■ Any penetrating wounds or cuts to the eye need specialist medical attention.

■ Orbital cellulitis is a very serious and potentially life-threatening condition. If any symptoms such as swollen eye lids, tenderness under the cheekbones or limited eye movement present themselves, urgent medical attention should be sought.

Chapter Five

Common Stomach and Urinary Problems

Simple anatomy and physiology

- The digestive system – This begins with the mouth, which contains teeth which chew and mix the food with salivary enzymes. These enzymes break down or digest foods (often referred to as carbohydrates, fats and proteins), allowing slow passage through the digestive tract, where the food is either absorbed into the body or eliminated as waste through the large bowel, rectum and anus. Many structures and organs are found within the abdominal cavity. These include the stomach, small intestine, large intestine, liver, spleen, pancreas, gall bladder and the kidneys.

- The urinary system – A bean-shaped pair of kidneys lie towards the back of the upper abdomen. The main functions of the kidneys are the filtration of blood, the formation of urine, the selective reabsorption of electrolytes and nutrients, and the elimination of water, excess electrolytes, waste products and by-products of drugs in the form of urine. The kidneys also have a role to play in the balance of internal body fluids, salts and potassium ions, the activation of vitamin D to promote healthy bones and teeth, the stimulation of red cell production and the maintenance of normal blood pressure and circulating blood volume.

What are common conditions and problems?

Diarrhoea and vomiting

Babies and young children can often suffer with diarrhoea and/or vomiting. Most often, the illness is caused by a viral infection, often picked up from other children at nursery or school. If your baby or child is otherwise well, it should settle over 24 hours.

If your child has other symptoms such as a fever, crying, or you are worried about dehydration, seek medical advice straight away. If you attend an appointment at your surgery, remember to take a sample of your baby's or child's stool with you in a sterile container. The doctor or nurse will be able to send it off for analysis. If you have been abroad recently, let your doctor or nurse know. If your surgery is shut, contact NHS Direct on 0845 4647 for advice.

'To treat diarrhoea at home, remember to increase fluid intake.'

To treat diarrhoea at home, remember to increase fluid intake. If your baby or toddler is breastfed, you can continue as normal. You can supplement fluids with extra drinks of water. You can purchase rehydration drinks from your pharmacy too. See chapter 11 for more details.

If your child is older, continue with increased fluids but don't force them to eat solids until their appetite has returned. Also, avoid cow's milk until 24 hours after the diarrhoea has resolved.

Vomiting can be due to viral infections, such as middle ear or throat infections, but also as a side effect of some medicines. To treat vomiting, continue to encourage fluids but give little and often, then gradually increase. Avoid solid food until your child is asking for food. If vomiting persists or if you are worried, contact your doctor or NHS Direct.

Signs of dehydration include:

- Dizziness or feeling light-headed.
- Headache.
- Tiredness.
- Dry mouth, lips or eyes.

- Passing small amounts of dark concentrated urine (less than four times in 24 hours).

Severe signs include:

- Very dry skin.
- Rapid or weak pulse or palpitation.
- Cold hands and feet.
- Seizures.

Any of the above can lead to seizures, kidney failure, coma and even death, and require immediate medical attention. If you are worried a simple test is to look in your child's mouth. Is the tongue and inside the cheeks moist or dry? If they are dry, you need to seek medical attention.

Colic

This condition is commonly identified when a baby cries and screams for long periods of time, possibly going red in the face and often drawing the knees up to the chest. This is distressing for any parents to witness but be assured that once the spasm has passed, your baby will settle again. Unfortunately, you cannot prevent your baby from developing colic. The cause is unknown but we do know that it settles, usually after three months of age.

You can ease your baby's suffering by rocking, burping or just cuddling. For severe cases, gripe water or infant colic drops have been found to help. Speak to your pharmacist or health visitor about this distressing problem.

Constipation

Constipation is very common, affecting all age groups. Dehydration during hot weather or fever can worsen the problem. The single most effective way of treating constipation is to encourage drinking more fluids. Exercise can play a part too.

'Constipation is very common, affecting all age groups. The single most effective way of treating constipation is to encourage drinking more fluids.'

To treat constipation, as well as increasing fluids, encourage a diet which includes a variety of fibre-rich foods (see chapter 8) such as fruit and vegetables. Stubborn constipation can be treated by your pharmacist with a mild laxative called syrup of figs. (See chapter 11 for details.) If the problem persists, you should discuss it with your health visitor, nurse practitioner or doctor.

Bad breath (halitosis)

Do not be alarmed if your child's breath smells, as this is a very common problem. Usual causes include dental disease, poor teeth brushing technique, foods containing garlic or spices, congestion causing dry mouth in the mornings and teenage secret smoking. From a medical cause, those suffering with frequent nose bleeds can suffer with bad breath, as can those suffering with sore throat or sinus infections. Foreign bodies stuck up a young child's nose may be a cause. A young teenager who is crash-dieting can suffer too.

To treat bad breath:

- Improve oral hygiene, clean with a good quality brush at least twice daily with a toothpaste containing fluoride. Buy a new brush every three to four months. It is best to brush before eating or at least an hour afterwards.

- Avoid sugary food and drinks as bacteria thrives on these. Also, they contribute to tooth decay and erosion. Also, limit fizzy and fruit drinks if you can.

- Remember to have regular dental check-ups.

- Use daily mouthwash. Cleaning the tongue with a soft brush using mouthwash is effective too.

- Encourage your child to drink plenty of water.

- If you suspect your child has an infection or a foreign body up the nose, see your doctor or nurse practitioner.

- Ensure medicines are sugar-free.

- If you suspect your child is smoking, you need to address this too. Your practice nurse or school nurse can advise you on how best to deal with this.

Oesophageal reflux

This is a common complaint in infants. Reflux is recognised as being non-forceful regurgitation of milk or gastric contents into the gullet. By twelve to eighteen months it usually resolves.

Severe cases are more common in children with cerebral palsy and Down's syndrome. The symptoms can range from reluctance to feed due to heartburn, pain on swallowing, irritability and sudden crying. Complications can include bleeding from the gullet, causing anaemia, failure to thrive, and respiratory problems such as apnoea and aspiration pneumonia. More worryingly, there has been some link between reflux and sudden infant death syndrome.

If you are concerned that your infant may have reflux problems, visit your GP who will be able to diagnose the condition. For milder cases, the doctor will advise more frequent, smaller feeds and nursing whilst the baby lies on the left side – a position which is known to help the condition.

If these measures do not help, medication to thicken feeds may be advised. Sometimes infant Gaviscon is prescribed to be mixed with feeds. Alternatively, your baby may need to be referred to a paediatrician for more expert advice.

Norovirus

Norovirus (the winter vomiting bug) is caused by a viral infection. Although more common in the winter, it can occur any time of the year.

'The virus is easily spread by contact with an infected person, especially through their hands. You can also catch it through contaminated food or drink or by touching contaminated surfaces or objects'. NHS Choices.

Symptoms include diarrhoea and vomiting but dehydration, headache, dizziness, aching limbs, cramps and passing small amounts of urine may also be present. There is no specific treatment apart from replacement of lost fluids by increasing fluid intake, taking rehydration sachets and paracetamol for control of pain and fever. Most people recover within a few days. Those most at risk from complications are the very young, the elderly and those who are immunosuppressed.

'Norovirus (the winter vomiting bug) is caused by a viral infection. Although more common in the winter, it can occur any time of the year.'

Here are some simple infection control measures to reduce the spread of disease:

- Thorough and frequent hand washing techniques, especially after going to the toilet and before preparing or eating food.

- Discourage nail biting and finger sucking.

- When flushing the toilet, put the lid down to reduce the spread of airborne germs.

- Use own towels and flannels.

- Use hand gels.

- Kiss children on the cheeks rather than the lips.

- Flush all tissues down the toilet or put in a lidded bin after use.

- Encourage your child to put their hand over their mouth and turn away from others when coughing or sneezing, followed by hand washing.

- Clean all surfaces and door handles regularly with a disinfectant. Bugs can live for several days on contaminated surfaces.

- Do not allow your child to go swimming until two weeks after the last episode of diarrhoea.

'Threadworms have a short lifespan. You can treat an infestation by encouraging your child to wash their hands after using the toilet, discourage nail biting or finger or thumb sucking.'

Threadworms

Threadworms are very common in children. If you look carefully, you can see tiny, white thread-like worms attached to your child's stool (poo). Also, they can be seen around or on the anus, where they lay their eggs. The predominant symptom is an itchy bottom which is often worse in the evening. If you suspect threadworms, take your child for an appointment with your doctor or nurse practitioner in the morning. Do not wash their bottom so that the doctor or nurse can take a saline swab around the anus and send it off for examination.

Thankfully, threadworms have a short lifespan. You can treat an infestation by encouraging your child to wash their hands after using the toilet, discourage nail biting or finger or thumb sucking. Keep your child's fingernails short. Ensure everyone in the household uses their own towel. Your child should wear pants or pyjama bottoms at night. A daily bath or shower will help too. Treating your child and the whole family is important. Your pharmacist will be able to advise you. See chapter 11 for more details.

Appendicitis

Acute (sudden) appendicitis is common, affecting children normally over the age of five. The appendix is a small part of the large bowel which is not useful to human life. It becomes inflamed, swollen, infected and can burst, leading to peritonitis. It normally presents suddenly with central abdominal pain, moving later to the lower right side. Fever also occurs with vomiting. This needs treating with surgery. If you suspect appendicitis, do not delay. Seek medical advice immediately.

Urinary infections and cystitis

These are far more common in girls compared to boys. In females, even with the best hygiene measures, germs can spread from the anus to the urethra, gaining access to the bladder. This can cause infections. If the germs are allowed to move from the bladder up to the kidneys, this can be very serious, causing pyelonephritis or renal failure and can be life-threatening if not treated.

In boys, the urethral entrance at the tip of the penis is much further away from the anus, so it is far more difficult for germs to gain access.

'Persistent bedwetting can affect your child psychologically, so it is important to seek advice.'

Bedwetting

Bedwetting is a common problem in young children, particularly under the age of five. Often no cause is identified and it will resolve itself without treatment. Sometimes, constipation or emotional stress such as bullying and changes at home can be the causative factor. Also bedwetting can sometimes be due to a urinary tract infection, especially more so in girls. It can also run in families.

If your child suffers with regular bedwetting, seek advice from your nurse, doctor or health visitor. Take a sterile urine sample with you so that it can be checked. Persistent bedwetting can affect your child psychologically, so it is important to seek advice.

Red flags! Seek medical attention urgently for any of the following:

- Severe worsening abdominal pain of any cause, this should be investigated by a medical professional.

- A persistent case of bad breath.

- Vomiting blood or blood in the stool, this needs urgent medical attention.

- Bile-stained vomit, this requires urgent assessment by a doctor.

- Signs of dehydration always require urgent assessment.

Summing Up

- Diarrhoea and vomiting affects people of all ages. It is often caused by viral infections and is normally contagious. It should usually settle down within 24 hours.

- A dry mouth, dry skin and dry lips added with confusion and listlessness are all signs of dehydration – increase your child's intake of fluid and if no improvement is seen seek medical attention urgently.

- The spread of many infections can be minimised by following simple infection control measures, which include frequent and thorough hand washing, especially before handling food and after using the toilet.

- Urinary tract infections are more common in girls. If you are concerned that your child has a urine infection, take them to see your doctor or nurse practitioner. Remember to take a sterile urine sample with you.

- Severe, worsening abdominal pain of any cause always needs medical attention, especially if there is fever and vomiting.

Chapter Six

Common Childhood Accidents and Emergencies

Sadly, accidents are one of the main causes of death among children between the ages of one and five. No matter how we try to protect our children, we cannot keep our eyes on them 24 hours a day. Children need to explore their surroundings in order to grow, develop and learn about their environment. By considering risks and taking steps to minimise them, we can dramatically reduce the chance and severity of dangerous events. Knowing what to do in the event of an accident reduces risks and saves lives. The issues related to accident prevention, road safety and safety in the home will be discussed within this chapter, where you will get lots of helpful and practical advice.

It is important to remind parents, grandparents, teachers, childminders and older children about the benefits of possessing effective resuscitation skills. Discussion of current resuscitation guidelines goes way beyond the scope of this book. However, you may wish to access up-to-date advice online at www. resus.org.uk/pages/guide.html. Also, *The First Aid Manual – Revised 9th Edition (2011)* published by Dorling Kindersley, is an excellent resource for you to take a look at. It has been written and authorised by the UK's leading first-aid providers: the British Red Cross, St Andrew's First Aid and St John Ambulance.

For those of you who would like to find out more about first-aid courses available, St John Ambulance and the British Red Cross provide regular courses in most areas of the UK. Visit www.sja.org.uk and www. redcrossfirstaidtraining.co.uk for more information.

'Knowing what to do in the event of an accident reduces risks and saves lives.'

Useful accident prevention measures for you and your family

Safety in the home

Against fire and electrocution

- Fit fire alarms on each level of your home. Test the batteries regularly.

- If you smoke, ensure all cigarettes are stubbed out properly.

- Switch all possible electrical appliances off at night and close all doors to stop fire from spreading.

- Use fire guards in front of open fires and heaters.

- Keep electrical appliances out of the bathroom.

- Fit socket covers on all unused electrical sockets.

- Contact your local fire station for more specific advice.

- Keep matches, lighters and fuels away from babies and children.

Bath time safety

- Never leave a baby or child alone in a bathroom, even if they are in a bath seat.

- To prevent scalding, always put the cold water in first and then add the hot. Mix thoroughly and test with your elbow. Comfortably warm is ideal.

- Cover the hot tap or mixer tap with a sock to prevent accidental burning if touched.

- Never leave older children in charge of younger ones.

Bedtime safety

- Never use duvets or pillows for babies under one year old. They can suffocate.

- Baby monitors are useful and offer reassurance when parents are in a different room.
- Never leave a baby alone in a cot with a bottle.
- Babies can climb out of cots by standing on toys. Take care.

Preventing falls

- Use baby gates at the top and bottom of the stairs and ensure they are installed safely.
- Never leave a baby unattended on a bed or sofa. Even very young babies can roll over and injure themselves.
- Bouncy cradles and car seats can move along any surface unnoticed. Place on the floor for safety.
- Try to keep the floor clear of toys. It is so easy to trip on a toy when carrying your baby or child or laundry basket. Your vision is impaired and you can trip.
- Keep the stairs clear too.
- Secure babies and small children correctly in a high chair or booster seat.
- Keep low furniture away from windows.
- Have window locks and safety latches fitted. Make sure all adults have easy access to the keys for quick access and escape in case of fire.
- Keep keys away from children.

Preventing poisoning

- Fit carbon monoxide alarms. This poisonous, odourless gas can kill.
- Ensure all gas appliances are serviced regularly.
- Ensure all ventilation outlets are not blocked.
- Keep all medicines out of reach in a locked cabinet or cupboard.
- Store all cleaning products in a locked cupboard too.

Kitchen safety

- Ensure children are never left alone while food is cooking.

- Make sure kettles are pushed well back and the cord is far from reach.

- Always have the pan handles pointing away from you.

- Do not leave hot drinks unattended.

Safety during play

- Only give age-appropriate toys to your baby or small child. Small toys to a baby or young child are a choking hazard.

- Never leave children alone during wet play in the garden. Drowning can occur in only a few inches of water. Ponds in the garden pose a huge risk.

Road and car safety

- All under fives must ride in a proper child safety car seat when travelling. Ensure the car seat is fitted correctly and is appropriate for your child's age, weight and size. Never purchase a second-hand car seat; its safety may have been compromised in a previous accident. You can get up-to-date advice from your local council.

- All children and babies under five, by law, must travel in the back seat.

- Never leave a baby or child in a car unattended. The car can become very hot, even on the coolest of days. Also, never leave the keys in the ignition.

- Ensure your child is aware of road safety issues at a young age. The risks increase once they start school, particularly when starting secondary school.

- Remind children not to use mobile phones, text messages, or listen to music when crossing the road. Even chatting to friends can be distracting and poses a risk. Familiarise your children at an early age with 'The Green Cross Code'.

What to do in the event of accident or injury

Anaphylactic shock

This is a severe allergic reaction which affects the whole body. Some people are allergic to foods such as nuts, shellfish, latex or eggs. Others are allergic to wasp and bee stings and some medications. Anaphylactic shock occurs from coming into contact with one of these triggers in susceptible people. It can develop in seconds or minutes and is potentially fatal. The blood vessels dilate, causing blood pressure to drop. The airways become narrow and the skin becomes pale or grey due to oxygen starvation.

Signs of anaphylactic shock include:

* Pale, clammy, cold skin which may rapidly turn grey/blue.

* Swelling of the lips, throat, tongue and the face.

* Rapid shallow breathing and a weak pulse.

* Weakness and dizziness.

* Nausea and vomiting.

* Restlessness or aggression due to oxygen starvation.

* Yawning or gasping.

* Collapse.

> If you suspect your child has gone into anaphylactic shock, it is vital that you call 999/112 and tell the operator that you suspect anaphylaxis.

In the event of anaphylactic shock, sit the child up to enable easier breathing. But if they become pale and start to sweat they are in shock and need to be lying down. If you can, lift the legs up. This will help improve the circulation. Try and keep the child calm. If the child has asthma, offer their usual reliever inhaler to relax the airways. The child in your care may be known to have allergies and may have emergency medicine in the form of an injectable drug

'Anaphylactic shock can develop in seconds or minutes and is potentially fatal. The blood vessels dilate, causing blood pressure to drop. The airways become narrow and the skin becomes pale or grey due to oxygen starvation.'

called adrenaline. If this is the case, the child may know how to use it, especially an older child. You can help them. If not, the emergency services on 999/112 will be able to talk you through what to do.

Accidental poisoning or overdose

Poisoning is when someone is exposed to or takes a drug or substance which is harmful to them and may put their life in danger.

- 12,000 people are hospitalised per year in England due to poisoning.

- The under fives are most at risk.

What you should do in a case of poisoning or overdose:

- If the child is not in danger, call NHS Direct on 0845 4647 for advice.

- If the child is vomiting, drowsy, fitting or losing consciousness, call 999 for an ambulance.

- If the child has the substance in the mouth, try and get them to spit out. *Never* make them vomit.

- Wipe away any vomit and put it in a container as this may help medical staff identify any poison.

- If there are any containers nearby which suggest these were the poisons taken, give the containers to the paramedic.

- Do not give anything to eat or drink.

'12,000 people are hospitalised per year in England due to poisoning.'

Bites

Animal bites

The most common causes of animal bites are dogs (80%), cats (15%) and humans (20%). Did you know that a human's mouth contains just as much bacteria as a dog's?

No matter how minor, all animal bites need assessing by a healthcare professional. Infection is a common complication. Normally, a course of antibiotics is required, even for human bites. Also, your doctor or nurse will want to make sure that your child is covered for tetanus.

Regarding first aid, wash the animal bite with running, warm water for at least a few minutes and squeeze the area to encourage bleeding. Then cover with a clean dressing or non-fluffy, clean piece of cloth. You can cover a wound with cling film too! Give simple painkillers such as ibuprofen or paracetamol (see chapter 11). If the bite is severe, such as a fingertip or ear having been bitten off, then wash the damaged appendage with warm water and put it in a sealed plastic bag. It may be reattached by a plastic surgeon.

Snake bites

Snake bites in the UK are uncommon. However, they still occur and it is important to know what to do. Also, you may be bitten whilst abroad on holiday and you need to be prepared.

Luckily, most snake bites are not serious and are rarely fatal. For all snake bites it is imperative that you seek medical attention fast by dialing 999 and asking for an ambulance. If you are abroad, you need to seek medical attention fast by visiting an accident and emergency department.

If you or your child is bitten by a snake . . .

Do:

- Try to remain calm.
- Try to recall what colour, shape and size the snake was and if it had any special markings.
- Keep the area that has been bitten very still.
- Carefully remove any jewellery around the bitten area.

Do not:

- Suck out the venom.

'No matter how minor, all animal bites need assessing by a healthcare professional. Infection is a common complication.'

- Rub anything into the wound.

- Apply a tight bandage or tourniquet.

- Try to catch or kill the snake.

Tick bites

Ticks and their bites are responsible for transmitting many infections, including lyme disease. Ticks look like tiny spider-like creatures. They attach to the skin and feed on the host. The bites are normally painless but can cause irritation and sometimes secondary infection.

Bites can be avoided. If you are travelling through a forested area, it is a good idea for your child to wear long trousers tucked well into boots such as wellies. Once you have left the area, check your child all over for ticks. If you find a tick, it needs prompt removal.

To remove a tick:

- Clean the surrounding skin first with a disinfectant cream such as Germolene cream or Savlon antiseptic cream.

- As close to the skin as possible, grasp the tick's mouth area gently with tweezers and pull steadily (do not twist).

- If you do not have tweezers, a loop of cotton put around the tick's mouth, close to the skin and pulled gently can be effective.

- If the skin becomes infected, you see a circular rash around the tick bite area or your child becomes unwell, seek medical attention.

> 'Cigarettes and glowing match heads or suffocating the tick with various agents (for example, petroleum jelly or solvents) are not recommended'. Web mentor library.

If not removed carefully, remnants can be left behind that can cause problems of infection and disease. Save the tick and place it in a sealed plastic bag. It is important to seek medical attention even though the tick is removed. Take the tick with you.

Burns

When the skin is burned, it is unable to provide an effective barrier against the elements and infection. Also, body fluid is lost through the affected area. Burns can be caused by scalds, electricity, household appliances such as irons, chemicals, radiation, cigarettes, friction, ropes and frostbite. Generally, a simple burn, however small, should be treated by a healthcare professional either at your surgery or at a minor injuries clinic. More severe burn victims should be transported to hospital urgently.

To treat a burn:

* Help the child to sit or lie down. They will be in some form of shock.

* If you can, gently remove any clothing, shoes, watches, jewellery that is not attached to the burn area before the area begins to swell.

* Cool the area with plenty of cold water. This reduces the damage and fluid loss to the burn site and helps relieve pain. If water is not available, you can use milk or canned drinks.

* Cover the burned area (so long as it is not on the face) with cling film to protect it from infection.

* Warm the child with blankets (carefully avoiding the burn). This will also help to treat shock and reduce the risk of hypothermia.

'When the skin is burned, it is unable to provide an effective barrier against the elements and infection.'

> Do not attempt to apply any creams, ointments or adhesive dressings to a burn. Also, no matter what you've heard, you should never put butter on burnt skin. It's important not to remove any clothing that is stuck to the skin.

Choking

This is caused through an object being stuck in the back of the throat which blocks the airways. In its mildest form, a simple cough will clear it. However, a severe blockage will cause the child to choke. They will not be able to speak, breathe or cough, which will lead to loss of consciousness.

If you suspect a child is choking:

- Lean the child well forward, support the front of the upper body with one hand, give up to five sharp slaps between the shoulder blades. This should dislodge the blockage.

- If back blows fail to clear the obstruction, you can do abdominal thrusts. Stand behind the child, put your arms around their upper body, ensure they are leaning well forward, put your fist between the belly button and breastbone and grasp your fist with your other hand. Now, pull upwards and inwards sharply up to five times. Stop when the obstruction clears. Also, remember to check the child's mouth.

- If you cannot clear the obstruction, you must call 999/112 for assistance. Continue to do the above whilst you are waiting for help.

Drowning

Once the child is pulled onto land, you need to follow the current resuscitation guidelines. These are very lengthy and go way beyond the scope of this book. However, this vital life-saving information can be found at www.nhs.uk/ conditions/pregnancy-and-baby/pages/resuscitating-a-baby.aspx.

Head injury

If your child shows any signs of the following, you need to phone 999 or 112 for an ambulance:

- Knocked out, loss of consciousness or fitting.

- Sick more than once.

- Difficulty in speaking or weak limbs.

- Blood coming from an ear.

- Watery discharge from the ears or nose or both.

Any of the following circumstances require you to take the child to A&E for assessment or ring NHS Direct on 0845 4647 for advice:

- A fall from a height higher than your child's height.

- If the child is under one year of age.

- If you suspect that it is an non-accidental injury.

If you feel the below circumstances fit more accurately, you can safely manage your child at home. You can give simple painkillers for any headache. See chapter 11 for more details.

- Your child is not knocked out.

- They cry immediately but only once and seem okay.

- They have a minor laceration or bruise.

- Vomits, but only once.

Knocked out tooth

If a secondary tooth (adult tooth) is knocked out, it may be re-implanted by a dentist or dental hospital. Place the tooth in a solution of milk – this prevents the tooth from drying out. Arrange an emergency appointment through your dentist or local dental hospital. Remember to take the tooth with you. Do not clean the tooth as this may cause damage.

Open wounds

A wound is just a break in the skin. There are many types of wounds which cause varying damage to the skin. Mild grazes and lacerations can be treated at home effectively with simple infection control measures, pressure and a simple dressing or plaster. More severe wounds will need medical attention.

To assess wound severity:

- Ask the child how they sustained the injury. This will help you in your assessment. Treat the child whilst they are sitting or lying down.

- Wash and dry your hands thoroughly. If you have access to disposable gloves, use these after washing and drying your hands. They will help prevent transfer of infection between you and the child.

'If a secondary tooth (adult tooth) is knocked out, it may be re-implanted by a dentist or dental hospital. Place the tooth in a solution of milk – this prevents the tooth from drying out.'

- Clean the wound with running cold water from the tap. You can also use an alcohol-free wipe, but do not use antiseptic cleansers as they may damage the surrounding skin.

- Gently pat the wound dry with a clean non-fluffy towel or cloth.

- Apply pressure to help stop the bleeding. So long as you're sure there isn't a fracture, elevating the limb is effective too.

- Apply a sterile dressing or a sticking plaster.

Seek medical attention if:

- The wound doesn't stop bleeding.

- It is a large or deep wound. (A knife wound or puncture wound may appear superficial but get it checked out – it could be deep with severe damage.)

- You suspect there is a foreign body within the wound.

- An old wound becomes more inflamed, more swollen or starts to weep.

- If the injury was caused by a human or animal bite.

- If you are worried.

- If you see large areas of bruising – this could be signs of widespread bleeding under the skin.

Always ensure that you ask how the child got the injury. This gives you information to help you decide if it is mild or more severe. If the bleeding continues you should attend your local minor injuries clinic or doctor's surgery.

Infection control matters

This needn't be complicated. Simple and effective hand washing goes a long way in preventing infection of wounds and preventing spreading illnesses and diseases such as flu, and diarrhoea and vomiting bugs. Effective cleaning of wounds is important.

Strains and sprains

These common injuries cause damage to the soft tissues – the ligaments, muscles and tendons. Injuries occur when these structures are overstretched. Sometimes they can be partially or completely torn, which may require surgery. Strains and sprains are often caused by sporting injuries.

You can treat minor sprains and strains using the RICE technique:

R – Rest the injured area

I – Apply an icepack or cold compress

C – Compress the injured area by using a bandage wrap to apply gentle but firm pressure.

E – Elevate the injured area.

It is necessary for you to take your child to a minor injury centre or to your doctor for assessment for review. You will not be able to assess if your child has a simple sprain or if he or she needs it correcting surgically. You can treat the area as above, but do not delay in seeking medical attention.

Wasp and bee stings

Stings from wasps, hornets and bees are normally more painful than dangerous. Once stung, sharp pain occurs, followed by mild swelling, some redness and discomfort. To treat a visible sting, do not try and pull it out with fingers or tweezers. This may squeeze the sting and cause more poison to enter the skin. Instead, brush the sting sideways with a credit card or your fingernail. You can treat the allergic reaction if it is mild with simple antihistamines. See chapter 11 for more details.

If your child is stung in the mouth or throat, this can lead to swelling and difficulty breathing. To treat this, give your child sips of cold water or if older, an ice cube to suck. If you suspect swelling, ring 999/112 for help.

Red flags! Seek medical attention urgently in the presence of:

- Severe swelling of a limb or joint.

- Excessive bleeding.

- Agitation or aggression.

- A suspected fracture.

- Loss of consciousness – however short term.

- Presence of severe pain.

- Electrical shock – however minor.

- Suspected overdose.

- Suspected seizure or fit.

- Suspected spinal injury.

- Severe burns.

Summing Up

* We can reduce the risks of severe injury and accidents by paying attention to safety issues in the home. This includes taking care during bath time, play, travelling by car and whilst cooking.

* Anaphylactic shock occurs when someone is exposed to an allergic trigger. It requires urgent medical attention and treatment.

* The under fives are most at risk of poisoning. Ensure all medicines and cleaning products are locked safely away.

* If your child's tooth is knocked out, take the child and tooth to a dental hospital. The dentist may be able to re-implant the tooth.

* Simple infection control measures will help reduce the risk of secondary infection when dealing with a minor burn or laceration.

* In the cases of any suspected overdose, poisoning, seizure, spinal injury or fracture/break seek medical attention immediately.

* Being aware of the effective treatment for burns helps reduce the chances of shock, infection and scarring.

Chapter Seven

Childhood Immunisations Explained

'It is now generally accepted that no other measure taken by Man, apart from the provision of clean water, has ever saved more lives than immunisation against infectious disease'. George C Kassianos, *Immunization: Childhood and Travel Health*.

In order to protect ourselves from infectious diseases, we develop immunity through our physical barriers; the skin and our mucus membranes and chemical barriers such as digestive enzymes and gastric fluid. We also acquire immunity over time. Our immune systems develop and mature in response to diseases and infections which we are exposed to in our daily lives.

We can also develop immunity through vaccination, which provides protection against infectious diseases without the risk of developing the disease or complications. Active immunity relates to protection that we develop within our own immune system having responded to either infection or a vaccine. Passive immunity relates to the protection we gain from either the transfer of antibodies from those already immune, our mother's immunity through the placenta (which tends to be temporary such as tetanus, polio, measles, whooping cough), or possibly transfusion of blood or blood products.

'Vaccines work by inducing active immunity and provide immunological memory. This "memory" allows the body to rapidly recognise exposure to an infectious disease and to respond to it by either preventing the disease process or modifying its behaviour.'

How do vaccines work?

Vaccines work by inducing active immunity and provide immunological memory. This 'memory' allows the body to rapidly recognise exposure to an infectious disease and to respond to it by either preventing the disease process or modifying its behaviour.

In other words, when you have a booster of a vaccine which you have already had previously, your memory cells rapidly boost up your immunity, within a couple of days in some cases. If you have a vaccine for the first time, it can take anything between ten days and three weeks to develop protection.

Also, small babies have a sluggish response to the usual baby vaccines, which is why they need to have vaccines repeated four weeks apart.

What is herd immunity?

When we are immunised, we gain protection against infectious diseases. Due to this, we then are no longer infectious to others, thus improving 'the herd immunity'. In other words, we as individuals benefit and so does the general population. This also means that those who cannot be vaccinated will still be protected.

What about consent issues?

Consent for immunisation needs to be given freely, where the person being offered immunisation is fully informed of the benefits, risks, side effects and possible complications.

Who has authority to give consent? This is where it may get tricky. The Children's Act 1989 states that mothers can automatically give consent. It is more complicated with fathers. If the father is married to the mother at the time of the child's birth, or he marries her subsequently then he has parental responsibility, therefore he too may give consent.

If the child was born after 1st December 2003 and the father is not married to the mother but is named on the birth certificate, he also has parental responsibility.

If you would like more information about consent issues, please read *Immunisation Against Infectious Disease 2011*, published by the Department of Health. It can also be freely downloaded or accessed online.

What vaccines are included in the current

'Consent for immunisation needs to be given freely, where the person being offered immunisation is fully informed of the benefits, risks, side effects and possible complications.'

childhood immunisation programme?

Normally, but not always, your practice nurse will give your child their vaccinations. The nurse will be fully informed and will attend mandatory regular training in order to be up to date and work safely. She will be able to answer any of your questions that you may have. Sometimes, she may need to call on the expertise of her local immunisation co-ordinator.

Vaccines available from birth to 14 years

- 2 months old – Diptheria, tetanus, pertussis (whooping cough), polio, hib; all combined in one injection and given in one thigh, pneumococcal given in the other thigh.

- 3 months old – Diptheria, tetanus, pertussis (whooping cough), polio, hib; all combined in one injection and given in one thigh. MenC given in the other thigh.

- 4 months old – Diptheria, tetanus, pertussis, (whooping cough), polio, hib; all combined in one injection and given in one thigh. MenC and pneumococcal each given as a separate injection in the other thigh.

- 12-13 months – Measles, mumps and rubella (MMR) given as one injection. Hib/MenC given as one injection and pneumococcal given as one injection. These are also given into the thighs.

- 3 years 4 months up to 5 years – Diptheria, tetanus, polio and pertussis as one injection. Measles, mumps and rubella (MMR) given as one injection. These are given into the upper arms.

- Girls aged 12-13 years – Human papillomavirus given as three separate injections at intervals into the upper arms.

- 13 to 18 years – Diptheria, tetanus and polio booster as one injection into the upper arm.

Vaccinations

Diptheria

Before the 1940s, diptheria was a common disease in the UK. Once immunisation began, there was a dramatic fall in numbers of those contracting the disease. Diptheria is still endemic in South-East Asia, South America, Africa and India. Travellers to these countries with waning immunity will be at risk.

Diptheria usually affects the upper respiratory tract. It causes a 'pseudo-membrane' across the back of the throat, fever, neck swelling and enlarged neck glands. The membrane can cause obstruction. Thankfully, this disease is now very rare. A milder form of the disease can look like a bacterial throat infection where the membrane does not develop. Diptheria can cause paralysis and heart attack. The incubation period is from two to five days, and the individual can be infectious for up to four weeks. Carriers who do not display any symptoms can be infective for longer.

Tetanus

Tetanus spores are present in soil and manure. We can become infected from this potentially fatal illness by transfer of spores through puncturing of the skin, a scratch or a burn. Newborn babies are especially at risk, particularly in countries such as Africa and Asia. The spores enter the body through the umbilical cord. Thankfully, due to an effective immunisation programme in these countries, there are far fewer cases.

The disease causes stiffness of the muscles and spasms. It is also known as 'lockjaw' for this reason. The incubation period can vary. The disease is a constant threat in all countries. As it is commonly found in soil, it can never be eradicated. This disease cannot be passed from person to person. Immunisation is imperative. It was first offered to the armed forces in 1938 and became widely available in 1961.

Pertussis (whooping cough)

This is a highly infectious disease caused by Bordetella pertussis. Following infection, the initial symptom is that of catarrh. This is followed by an irritating cough which within two to three weeks develops into paroxysms or prolonged, violent coughing spasms. These paroxysms are often followed by a 'whoop' sound. Some people may then vomit. The illness can last up to three months.

Complications can occur, such as pneumonia or brain damage due to oxygen starvation. Sadly, in infants under six months, death can occur. The disease is passed on through 'droplet infection', such as coughing and sneezing. The most infectious stage is the catarrhal stage. The incubation period is between six and twenty days.

Immunisation against pertussis began in the 1950s. Before this, the number of cases per year in the UK were around 120,000. Around 1975, many parents lost confidence in the vaccine and opted not to immunise their children. This resulted in a fall in the uptake rate of the vaccine by 30%, resulting in major epidemics occurring between 1977 to 1979 and 1981 to 1983. There were 14 deaths in 1978. Thankfully, since 1990, confidence has grown in the vaccine and the uptake rate has consistently remained at 90%.

Polio

This paralysing disease enters the body through the digestive system, through infected faeces or phlegm. It replicates in the intestines and is spread through the bloodstream to the nervous system, where it damages specific nerves. Symptoms present with fever, headache, abdominal upset, general malaise and stiff neck and back. Paralysis then follows.

The incubation period is between three and 21 days. Cases are most infectious just before and immediately after paralysis occurs. In the 1950s there were around 8,000 notified cases per year. Effective immunisation with a live vaccine was introduced in 1956. Cases fell rapidly and between 1985 and 2002 only 40 cases were reported.

Initially, a live vaccine was used, but as cases have dropped so dramatically, in 2004 a killed vaccine was introduced into the UK immunisation programme.

'Pertussis (whooping cough) is passed on through "droplet infection", such as coughing and sneezing. The most infectious stage is the catarrhal stage. The incubation period is between six and twenty days.'

Haemophilus influenzae type B (Hib)

Hib can cause serious illness, particularly in young children. It presents more commonly as meningitis, sometimes causing epiglottitis, which can cause breathing difficulties and is potentially fatal. It can also present as septic arthritis, osteomyelitis (infection within the bones), cellulitis (infection of the soft tissues), pneumonia and infection of the pericardium, a membrane surrounding the heart. Some people can carry the disease in the nose and throat without being affected. The disease is transmitted from person to person through droplet infection, for example sneezing or coughing. It can be caught from carriers through close contact, for example kissing. The Hib vaccine was introduced into the UK in 1992, where cases fell dramatically. However, cases began to increase among children born between 2000 and 2001. Therefore, a booster campaign was introduced in 2003, where cases fell again. Now a booster of Hib/MenC has been included in the immunisation schedule for those aged 12-13 months old.

'The meningococcal bacteria can live in the throat of carriers, without themselves becoming unwell.'

Additionally, adults and children who have had removal of their spleen are more at risk of developing infections, including Hib. For this reason, the vaccine is offered to them outside of the normal schedule.

Meningococcal C (MenC)

The MenC vaccine protects against infection by meningococcal group C bacteria, which can cause meningitis and septicaemia.

Meningitis is caused by the bacterium Neisseria meningitidis. There are at least 13 known subtypes, where group B and C are the most common in the UK. The disease presents as either meningitis or septicaemia or both. Less frequently, it can present in other forms, including pneumonia, infections of the heart muscles, conjunctivitis or arthritis.

The incubation period is between two and seven days. Symptoms present as general malaise, fever, vomiting, headache, stiff neck, dislike of the light, confusion or drowsiness. Sometimes joint pains or pains in the limbs can occur. A bruise-like rash may develop.

The meningococcal bacteria can live in the throat of carriers, without themselves becoming unwell. This can occur in up to 25% of young people. Those living in close-knit communities such as university accommodation seem to be more at risk. Also, children from birth up to five years old are more at risk. Sadly, the death rate runs at 10% in the UK, where fatal cases are higher in the group C cohort.

The MenC vaccine was introduced into the childhood immunisation programme in 1999. All those under the age of 18 were immunised. In 2002, all under 25s were offered the vaccine too. Following this new vaccine, cases fell by 90%. In 2006, a booster at aged 12 months was introduced into the childhood immunisation schedule.

Meningitis affects all countries. However, the 'meningitis belt' of the Sub-Saharan Africa is high risk. Please visit chapter 9 for more details.

Pneumococcal (PCV)

Pneumococcal disease is caused by the bacterium streptococcus pneumoniae. The incubation period is up to three days. The disease can spread through the throat into the sinuses and middle ear, causing sinusitis or middle ear infection. It can also spread to the lungs causing pneumonia and to the brain, resulting in meningitis. The bacteria is transmitted through droplet infection with peak levels in the winter months. Those at particular risk are the very young and the elderly, and those with cochlear implants, impaired immunity or skull fractures.

The PCV vaccine offers protection against 13 subtypes, which most commonly affect young babies and children. Rates of disease have dramatically fallen since Prevenar 7 was introduced in 2006 and then Prevenar 13 which was introduced in 2010.

Measles, mumps, rubella (MMR)

Measles is a viral disease which presents with symptoms of fever, general malaise, runny nose, conjunctivitis and a cough. A pale, flat, pink/red rash occurs which shows firstly on the head, spreading to the trunk, arms and legs over three or four days. Red spots with bluish-white centres may occur inside the mouth.

'Measles is a highly contagious disease. Common complications include middle ear infections, pneumonia, diarrhoea, fits or convulsions and encephalitis (infection of the linings of the brain). In the UK, death occurs in 1 in 5,000 cases.'

The disease is spread by droplet infection. The case is infectious from the start of the symptoms until four days after the rash appears. Measles is a highly contagious disease. Common complications include middle ear infections, pneumonia, diarrhoea, fits or convulsions and encephalitis (infection of the linings of the brain). In the UK, death occurs in 1 in 5,000 cases.

Mumps is a virus which causes swelling to the sides of the neck, either one side or both. For several days before the swelling, symptoms can include fever, headache, general malaise, appetite loss and muscle aches. It is spread through airborne or droplet infection. The incubation period is around 17 days. Infectious stages are from seven days prior to swelling and for up to seven days after. Complications of mumps include meningitis, pancreatitis, orchitis (swelling of the testicles), deafness and heart and kidney disease.

Rubella is a mild disease. Symptoms include fever, malaise, conjunctivitis and a runny nose. Swollen glands around the neck can occur and then a red rash, which is found usually behind the ears and on the face and neck. Again, the disease is spread through droplet infection. The incubation period is between 14 and 21 days. Cases are infectious from one week before the symptoms present until four days after the rash appears.

Complications are rare but include a blood disorder called thrombocytopenia, encephalitis and arthritis. More worryingly, if a woman contracts rubella any time up to 20 weeks of pregnancy, the risks are huge to her unborn child, particularly if she develops the disease in her first eight to ten weeks, whereby risk runs at 90%. The birth defects include cataracts, deafness, growth retardation, heart defects, including lesions to the brain, lungs, bone marrow and liver.

The MMR vaccine, introduced in 1988, offers safe, effective protection against measles, mumps and rubella. As a single dose of MMR will offer only 90% protection, a booster is required to increase immunity. This is why a booster was introduced into the immunisation schedule in October 1996. Due to this booster, teenage schoolgirls stopped getting the disease. Before a booster was introduced, mini-epidemics occurred every five years. The booster offers much improved herd immunity.

Human papillomavirus (HPV)

There are over 100 strains of human papillomavirus currently detected. Some cause warts on the hands and verrucas on the feet. Some are sexually contracted and cause warts to the genitals of women and men. Genital warts are the most common sexually transmitted infection in the UK today. Risks are increased in those who smoke, start sexual activity at an early age or have multiple partners. If left alone, 90% of infections will resolve within two years. Reassuring? Yes, but there is a very worrying concern about cervical and penile cancer.

According to the Department of Health Green Book, HPV has been found to be an indicator in the development of both cervical and penile cancers; infections increasing in mid-teens. Thankfully, in 2008 two vaccines were launched; both highly effective in offering protection against HPV. A course of three injections over a period of six months is offered to girls over the age of 12, hopefully long before they are sexually active. Having the vaccines early means that they will be protected when they start to become sexually active. Also, they cannot spread it to their partners so therefore this reduces the risk of penile cancers. The vaccine is not routinely offered to girls over the age of 18.

'Coughs and colds, so long as your child remains well with no fever, are not reason to delay vaccine.'

Vaccine contraindications, common side effects and their management

When you take your baby or child to the immunisation clinic, the nurse will ask if your child has a fever or has been known to have a previous reaction to any vaccine. If your answer is no, then there is no need for your child to be excluded from vaccination. Coughs and colds, so long as your child remains well with no fever, are not reason to delay vaccine.

Whatever the vaccine, the normal side effects include soreness, redness or mild swelling at the injection site for up to 48 hours. Also, your child may develop a fever. All of these mild side effects can be treated with either paracetamol or ibuprofen. Please view chapter 11 for more details. If your child has a fever, reduce their clothing and remember to increase their normal fluid intake to prevent the risk of dehydration.

Red flags! What you should do next

Any child that screams for hours following a vaccine should be reviewed by a doctor. I'm happy to say that this is rare, and any distress through pain is normally treated successfully with paracetamol or ibuprofen.

Also, any severe swelling or heat to the affected limb should be seen promptly by a health professional. If the surgery is shut, contact NHS Direct for advice or ring your casualty department. Alternatively, if you ring your surgery, there should be an answer phone message, informing you of where you can access advice out of hours. Similarly, your surgery may have a website where you can access this information.

For any child who develops facial swelling, wheezing or difficulty in breathing, severely swollen eyes, faints, becomes sweaty or grey, this is a medical emergency, displaying signs of a severe allergic reaction called 'anaphylaxis'. You should ring for an ambulance without delay.

Nowadays, we take immunisation for granted, some parents even decide not to immunise their children due to concerns about side effects or worries that vaccines have not been tested thoroughly before being added to the immunisation programme.

Rest assured that childhood immunisation saves lives. This is a fact. Certainly, if you have concerns or worries then it is imperative that you seek information and advice. For you to give informed consent, you need to be sure that you are happy for your baby or child to receive any vaccine. Any doctor, nurse or health visitor will be happy to explain the benefits of immunisation. Also, for really tricky questions that they may not be able to answer right away, they always have an expert to contact for more information.

Summing Up

- Our skin and mucus membranes provide a physical barrier to infection. This protection is further supported by our immune system.

- Active immunity is developed through a response to previous infection or through vaccination.

- A robust herd immunity helps to protect those individuals who, for whatever reason, are unable to receive vaccinations.

- Informed consent from a parent or legal guardian must be obtained before a child can receive their immunisations.

- A practice nurse normally administers immunisations to children under the age of five, where the school nurse takes over this task for school-aged children.

- Vaccines administered from birth to late teens include the combined injection of diptheria, tetanus and whooping cough; MenC and pneumococcal; MMR and the HPV vaccination.

- Common side effects to vaccines include mild fever, redness, swelling and mild pain to the injection site, where paracetamol is usually all that is required.

Chapter Eight

Diet and Nutrition for Healthy Growth and Development

Infant feeding

The World Health Organisation (WHO) recommends that 'All mothers should have access to skilled support to initiate and sustain exclusive breastfeeding for 6 months and ensure the timely introduction of adequate and safe complementary foods with continued breastfeeding up to two years or beyond'. www.webmentorlibrary.com

However, I'm sure you will agree that this is a matter of choice for new mothers.

Research from 2005 showed that the highest incidence of breastfeeding was found amongst the following groups:

▦ Mothers from professional or managerial employment.

▦ Those aged 30 and over.

▦ First-time mothers.

The advantages for babies who are breastfed are:

▦ A breastfed baby has lower rates of infection due to protection from the mother's mature immunity.

▦ Babies tend to become less constipated.

'A breastfed baby has lower rates of infection due to protection from the mother's mature immunity.'

- Exclusive breastfeeding has been shown to reduce the incidence of asthma and eczema.
- Breastfeeding is protective against sudden infant death syndrome.
- It has been suggested that breastfed babies appear to have a higher IQ.
- Obesity levels at aged four are reduced amongst those who are breastfed.

The advantages to breastfeeding mothers are:

- Breastfeeding reduces the chance of the mother developing breast cancer.
- It can be used as an effective form of contraception when the baby is under the age of six months.

Disadvantages of breastfeeding are:

- HIV-positive mothers can transmit the HIV infection to their baby through breast milk. Other infections such as influenza, TB and group B streptococci and staphylococci can be transmitted too.
- Cracked nipples and mastitis are common problems.
- Some drugs can be transmitted via breast milk.

'Your baby requires milk for the first twelve months of life. Mothers are encouraged to start weaning when baby turns six months of age.'

Introducing solids or weaning

Your baby requires milk for the first twelve months of life. Mothers are encouraged to start weaning when baby turns six months of age.

Smooth purees of root vegetables and fruit such as carrot, parsnip, potato, banana, cooked apples or pears are ideal. Initially, a teaspoon of any of these can be mixed with your baby's usual milk. This can be offered either at the beginning or during a normal milk feed.

Always avoid salt, honey and sugar.

In-depth advice in relation to the dietary requirements of babies and small children goes way beyond the scope of this book as it is a speciality in itself. You can get expert and up-to-date advice concerning breastfeeding from your midwife and weaning from your health visitor.

Vitamin D deficiency: who is at risk?

Vitamin D deficiency reduces the absorption of calcium and phosphorus from our diet which is essential for the development of healthy bones and teeth. The Department of Health are concerned that there are some people living in the UK who are at risk of developing vitamin D deficiency. Those at risk are: pregnant women, young children and infants, children under the age of five, the elderly over the age of 65 and those who avoid exposure to the sun, particularly those who, for cultural reasons, are totally covered by clothing. Also, darker skinned people need more sunlight in order to absorb the sun's rays.

Recommendations

The NHS recommends that those over 65 and all pregnant and breastfeeding mothers should have a daily supplement of vitamin D. Also, all infants and young children should have a daily supplement too. Why not speak to your doctor or health visitor for up-to-date advice.

What about iron supplements?

Babies have enough iron stores to last until they are six months old. After this, they need to obtain iron stores from their diet. Iron is crucial for the development of healthy red blood cells, which aid oxygen stores to reach all parts of the body. Lack of iron can cause developmental retardation of the baby's brain and can expose the baby or toddler to more infections.

Try to give your baby or child foods that are rich in iron, such as green vegetables like broccoli, spring cabbage, white and brown bread, lean red meat, peas, baked beans and breakfast cereals. Did you know that if you can encourage your child to drink fluids rich in vitamin C, this will increase iron absorption? Remember to always consult your health visitor for age-appropriate advice.

What is the impact of obesity in childhood?

Obesity in childhood increases the child's risk of being obese as an adult. If one parent is obese, the child has a 20-40% risk of becoming obese. If both parents are obese, the child is 80% more likely to become obese. Obesity has a direct impact on health, increasing the risk of developing life-threatening conditions such as diabetes, heart disease, impaired fertility, high blood pressure, breathing problems and some cancers. Not only that, it can lead to depression and low self-esteem. The World Health Organisation adds that obesity is more of a health threat than smoking.

If you are concerned that your child has a weight problem and you would like help, visit your nurse or doctor at your surgery. Alternatively, you could contact your health visitor or school nurse for advice.

So why is obesity becoming such a problem?

Interestingly, research has shown that food adverts have a direct effect on children. Did you know that, according to research, your child's dietary intake can rise 130% after watching food adverts on TV? To add to the problem, children eat more nowadays whilst exercising far less. Our children stay at home, often playing on their computers or watching TV for hours. They tend to eat high-fat, energy-dense foods compared to children, say 50 years ago.

What other causes can encourage overeating?

Did you know that eating habits can be affected by emotional and psychological issues? Often unhappiness can lead to overindulgence. If you suspect that your child has any worries, try and get to the bottom of it. Has there been a family bereavement, marital breakdown or change in environment? Is your child being bullied at school?

Helen Croker, BSc (Hons) says, 'Solving the problem of overweight in children usually involves lifestyle changes, not just for the child but for the whole family.' Often help with food-related behaviour can make a huge difference.

'Obesity has a direct impact on health, increasing the risk of developing life-threatening conditions such as diabetes, heart disease, impaired fertility, high blood pressure, breathing problems and some cancers.'

Generally speaking, the focus on children is not for them to lose weight, rather through healthy eating and increased exercise, they will 'grow into their weight' as they become taller. Try and focus on a balance between good nutrition and regular fun exercise.

To increase activity for the whole family perhaps you could try to:

- Reduce TV watching or computer games to two hours or less.
- Encourage regular fun activities which you and your child can enjoy. As a guide, your child should aim for one hour of exercise per day.
- Take up a new sporting hobby that the whole family can enjoy.
- Exercise outside so that you can all enjoy the benefits of fresh air, sunshine and exercise.
- Walk the dog (if you have one) together, dog walking is great exercise that the whole family can enjoy.
- Walk to the shops instead of driving, this can be fun too. You will meet people whilst out walking.

To reduce calorie intake:

- Try loading your child's plate with fruit or vegetables before adding the remainder of the meal. This will provide a better balance and encourage their five-a-day.
- Try encouraging fruit in-between meals if you or your child fancies a snack.
- Try drinking more water as this may satisfy rather than eating something.
- Try eating regular meals at the table to encourage routine.
- Try eating from smaller plates.
- Replace sugary drinks for water and low-calorie drinks.
- Encourage your children to eat more slowly and to chew properly.
- Try and avoid 'food on the run'.

If you are overweight and you wish to address this:

- Identify your own feelings about food and why you are eating at any given time. How could you be more health conscious?

'The focus on children is not for them to lose weight, rather through healthy eating and increased exercise, they will "grow into their weight" as they become taller.'

- Make a food-related plan of action, setting a date to implement this. Try to think about how you will deal with any obstacles that may occur.

- Use 'positive imagery'. For example, try and visualise how your life will be improved once you have achieved your goal.

- Writing a record of your food intake, exercise and monitoring your weight regularly can keep you positive.

- Avoid shopping when you are hungry. Don't walk past the takeaway shop if you know you will be unable to resist.

- Plan healthy meals in advance. Remember to write a shopping list.

- Regular non-food related rewards work too. For example, why not buy your child a new football if he has kept to the plan; a new CD for yourself?

- Try and get support from family and friends. You never know, they may wish to join in too.

- Remember, kids learn by example. If you have a healthy relationship with food, they will too.

Where can I go for expert advice?

Detailed information about child nutrition goes way beyond the scope of this book but you can access help from a wide range of sources.

Change 4 Life run an up-to-date, healthy eating and lifestyle programme which encourages eating well, moving more to live longer. Change 4 Life is an NHS-led initiative which involves the whole family. As well as promoting healthy eating to reduce the risk of obesity-led illnesses, they organise local events and activities all over the country. You can access load of interesting ideas, recipes and information at www.nhs.uk/change4life.

Slimming World also offer a service to children aged between 11 and 15. These children can attend free if they attend with a fee-paying adult. Slimming World provide an excellent eating programme and a sensitive and caring approach to weight loss for members. See the help list for more details.

You can access a 36-page booklet written by the NHS called *Your Weight, Your Health*. Here you will have access to loads of helpful tips on diet and exercise, and behavioural changes.

Also, you can visit your GP or practice nurse for advice. If you wish, your GP will be able to refer you or your child to a local dietician. Similarly, your pharmacist may be able to give you advice.

Healthy eating tips

- Swap sugary snacks with fruit.

- Kids need smaller meals than adults.

- Eat regularly as a family.

- Keep snacks to a minimum.

- Remember your 'five-a-day'.

- Try and reduce fat wherever you can.

- Aim for one hour of exercise per day.

Summing Up

- There are advantages and disadvantages to breastfeeding for you and your baby but the general consensus is that 'breast is best'. This view is supported by the World Health Organisation.

- Weaning your baby is safe from the age of six months. Don't forget that baby needs ample quantities of milk for the first twelve months of life.

- Start weaning by offering puree cooked root vegetables and fruit. You can mix these with your baby's usual milk too.

- Never give your baby added sugar, salt or honey.

- Those at risk of developing vitamin D deficiency include the very old, the very young, those who avoid the sun, pregnant women and people with dark skin.

- Vegetables such as broccoli, spring cabbage, peas and beans, bread and lean red meat are a great source of iron, essential for the formation of healthy red blood cells.

- Obesity runs in families and increases the risk of developing heart disease, diabetes, hypertension and all cancers.

Chapter Nine

Travel Health for the Family

When planning a holiday, probably the last thing on your mind is the possibility of illness or accidents. Fortunately, with a bit of careful planning, many illnesses and accidents are avoidable. Knowing what to do if the worst occurs is the key to minimising risk and spoiling your holiday.

This chapter deals with tourist and package type holidays. Unfortunately, dealing with backpacking and trekking holidays goes beyond the scope of this book. For more detailed information in relation to higher risk travel, check out www.fitfortravel.nhs.uk and www.patient.co.uk/doctor/Flying-with-Medical-Conditions.htm.

We will look briefly at vaccine-preventable illnesses specific to travel, and some medications that you may wish to take with you to treat minor illnesses. More details regarding the UK vaccination schedule can be found in chapter 7. Also, further advice regarding over the counter medicines can be found in chapter eleven.

For those who are pregnant, the safest time to travel is between the 14th and 28th week of pregnancy. Travelling outside of these weeks, you may have a higher risk of the need for medical attention. If you are at all concerned, please check with your midwife before you book your holiday.

Why are travel vaccines important?

Although your travel operator may suggest that you do not require travel vaccines to enter a country, you still need to visit your practice nurse or local travel clinic to find out what your specific health and immunisation needs may be. Your child's normal immunisation programme will offer protection against diptheria, tetanus, polio, meningitis Group C, hib, MMR, TB and pneumonia.

Common travel vaccines which may be required for travel are hepatitis A, hepatitis B and typhoid. Less common vaccines include yellow fever, tick-borne encephalitis and rabies. Your practice nurse will be able to advise you regarding which vaccines you and your family require. When receiving vaccines from your practice nurse, she can offer a vaccine record card where all your vaccines can be recorded. You can keep this for your own reference.

'Although your travel operator may suggest that you do not require travel vaccines to enter a country, you still need to visit your practice nurse or local travel clinic to find out what your specific health and immunisation needs may be.'

What happens at your travel clinic appointment?

It is important that you attend any travel appointment at least six weeks prior to travel. It can take up to three weeks for your body to develop immunity once immunised. Some vaccines, such as rabies, need to be started at the latest, four weeks prior to travel. Following, you can read about common travel vaccines. Visit chapter 7 for information about the normal childhood immunisation schedule for the UK

Travel vaccines

Diptheria, tetanus and polio (DTP)

DTP vaccines are routine vaccinations for all ages in Britain. They are given as a combination injection. Once completed the primary course, you should have a booster every ten years regardless of travel. The boosters provide ten years of protection. This vaccine is freely available on the NHS. Please visit chapter 7 for more details.

Hepatitis A & B

Hepatitis (inflammation of the liver) can be caused by hepatitis A, hepatitis B and hepatitis C. You can get protection from both hepatitis A and hepatitis B. Hepatitis A is transmitted through infected food and water, especially seafood. Hepatitis B and hepatitis C are contracted through infected body fluids such as semen and blood. They can also be transmitted by using dirty needles and syringes. You can protect yourselves with a course of hepatitis B vaccines. Currently, there are no available vaccines for protection against hepatitis C.

To provide further protection, it is a good idea to purchase a sterile medical kit from any good chemist. These contain sterile needles, syringes and sutures (stitches) which you may need. If you need medical treatment and you are not sure of the sterility of the local instruments, then you can ask the medics to use yours. Although hepatitis A vaccines are freely available on the NHS, you most probably will be charged a sum of money for hepatitis B vaccines as they are not available on the NHS.

Typhoid

Typhoid fever can be transmitted through the faecal/oral route. Even if a restaurant is very clean and hygienic, if the chef is a typhoid carrier, he or she can pass the disease through preparing your food. Luckily, you can be protected through vaccination. However, the vaccine is not 100% effective so you still need to ensure that you are careful. Typhoid vaccine is freely available on the NHS.

Rabies

If you are travelling to a high-risk area, backpacking, or staying in rural areas that are high risk, you could catch rabies if you are bitten, scratched or licked by an animal who is infected by the disease. Remember, rabies is universally fatal, and it can take up to two years to die once infected.

'If you are travelling to a high-risk area, backpacking, or staying in rural areas that are high risk, you could catch rabies if you are bitten, scratched or licked by an animal who is infected by the disease.'

If your nurse advises that you have a rabies vaccine, you will develop immunity but will still need a booster within 24 hours if bitten, scratched or licked on a wound. You will also have to pay for this injection as it is not available on the NHS.

Yellow fever

This vaccine is recommended if you are travelling to an endemic destination, especially if rural areas are visited. Yellow fever is caught through being bitten by mosquitoes carrying the disease. If yellow fever vaccination is required for travel, you will need a vaccination certificate to show that you have been immunised. Yellow fever vaccination can only be obtained from a designated 'yellow fever centre'. Again, your practice nurse will be able to advise you on this.

Cholera

Cholera immunisation is less effective. Most travellers are at very low risk of contracting cholera. If you are travelling to a country where cholera is endemic, then you are able to protect yourself by careful food and water hygiene measures.

Tick-borne encephalitis

This disease exists in Scandinavia and across central and Eastern Europe and Western Russia. It is transmitted through a tick bite. 90% of those bitten do not develop any symptoms but 10% develop encephalitis – a dangerous disease causing inflammation of the brain tissue. You are most at risk if you are camping, trekking or walking through endemic rural areas. Risk is greatest between the months of April to October. The disease can be transmitted through unpasteurised dairy products.

You can prevent this disease through immunisation and taking care to only use pasteurised dairy products. You need to start immunisation at the latest, a month before travel at a private travel clinic. There will also be a charge as it's not available on the NHS.

Please visit chapter 6 for details on how to safely remove a tick.

Meningitis ACYW-135

Meningitis is endemic in Sub-Saharan Africa, particularly in the dry, dusty season. You are also at high risk if travelling to Mecca in Saudi Arabia. Disease is predominantly from serogroup A, although cases of W-135 have been reported. You can receive immunisation against these forms of meningitis with a vaccine from your travel clinic. The vaccine offers up to five years of protection.

Insect bites

It is important to be aware that you can be bitten or stung from an array of insects, including flying insects, mites, ticks, mosquitoes, bees and wasps. Most insects do not cause harm, although many can pass disease to those bitten.

Insect bites generally cause localised redness, heat, itching, swelling and sometimes pain. This is usually due to an allergic reaction, but sometimes infection can occur. Secondary infection is most likely in tropical countries but not always. It most often occurs 48 hours following the bite. Signs of infection include increased pain, swelling and redness, which may track up the limb or become more widespread. Pus can occur, as can fever. You must seek medical attention if concerned.

To protect against mosquitoes and other insects:

- Cover the skin during dawn and dusk with lightweight clothing – long sleeves and long trouser legs can be very effective too.

- Try to book accommodation which provides air-conditioning and screens on doors and windows.

- Sleep under a mosquito net that has been treated with insecticide. Reapply frequently.

- The best insecticide is 'DEET' and can be bought from any good chemist in the form of creams, sticks, roll-ons and sprays.

'You and your family are at risk of catching malaria if you are visiting the tropics or sub-tropics. Malaria is a life-threatening disease which is preventable.'

Malaria

You and your family are at risk of catching malaria if you are visiting the tropics or sub-tropics. Malaria is a life-threatening disease which is preventable. The World Health Organisation suggests that there are up to 500 million cases of malaria each year.

There are a number of different forms of malaria, each requiring different prophylactic (preventative) treatment. Chloroquine and proguanil can be purchased over the counter, but others, such as doxycycline, mefloquine and Malarone are only available on private prescription from your surgery or local private travel clinic. Malaria tablets work by preventing the parasite from establishing itself in the blood and liver cells. It is important to remember that you also need to use insect repellents as none of the tablets are 100% effective.

The incubation period for malaria is between nine and sixteen days usually, but it can be much longer.

On return from your holiday, if any of you develop a fever at night, flu-like symptoms, joint pains or develop jaundice, please see you doctor as soon as possible.

You can easily check if you are at risk by accessing www.fitfortravel.nhs.uk online and entering your destination. The page will give you access to a malaria map and it will indicate, using an easy colour coding system, if you are at risk.

Food and water hygiene

Did you know that most food and water-borne illnesses are spread through water or food contaminated by faeces? You are more at risk if you visit countries where local hygiene standards are low. The best way to reduce risk is to ensure that you eat food that is cooked fully and eaten straight away. Avoid food from local markets or stalls. If a restaurant is quiet, avoid it. The food may not be freshly prepared and may be reheated regularly. If you are eating fruit, ensure it has been peeled properly.

Take great care with drinks too. Use only bottled water for drinking. Also, remember to brush your teeth with bottled water and avoid ice cubes in drinks too. Remember, pasteurised and long-life milk is safe to drink. Drinking glasses can be contaminated with local water so if you can, drink straight from the bottle or can, but make sure you wipe it first. Ensure that you and your family are well hydrated at all time, especially in hot weather. Also, insist that your family regularly use hand wipes. This will reduce any risk.

'Take great care with drinks too. Use only bottled water for drinking. Also, remember to brush your teeth with bottled water and avoid ice cubes in drinks too.'

Sun protection

'In 2006, more than 90,000 people were diagnosed with skin cancer in the UK' and 'Each year 2,600 people die from skin cancer'. NHS Choices.

Nowadays, we are far more aware of the damaging effects of the sun's rays on unprotected skin and the links to skin cancer but we can still get caught out. It's all about enjoying the sun safely. Additionally, overexposure to the sun can cause dehydration and sunstroke. The very young and the elderly are at increased risk.

Antimalarials called doxycycline can make you more prone to burning too! Overexposure to the sun's rays can lead to premature skin ageing and possible skin cancer, but complete protection can lead to vitamin D deficiency, so it's all about a healthy balance.

Points to consider

- You are more at risk of sunburn between the hours of 10am and 3pm; midday being high risk.

- Wear a T-shirt in the water.

- Don't forget tops of feet which burn easily. Wearing waterproof shoes for extra protection in the pool helps. They also reduce the chance of slipping on the tiled surfaces around the pool edge.

- Always apply good quality sun block which protects against UVA and UVB sun rays, starting at high factor, reducing over time, also, apply frequently. Don't forget tops of ears, shoulders and forehead.

- Wear a hat with a brim.

- Don't forget, you can get sunburnt when the sun reflects off snow, so use sun creams when on skiing holidays too.

Treatment for sunburn

You can use Sudacrem which helps soothe and protect burnt skin. Also, do not break any blisters. Anti-inflammatories and paracetamol can be used to ease pain. Increase fluid intake to help reduce dehydration. Aloe vera creams have been shown to help with soothing and healing sunburnt skin. Burns that are painless indicate that they are severe and must receive urgent medical attention. Extensive blistering also requires urgent medical attention. See chapter 11 for more details.

What are common holiday illnesses and accidents?

Fires

Once settled in your hotel, ensure that all of your family are aware of where the fire exits are located. If you smoke, never smoke in bed and ensure that your cigarette is stubbed out completely.

Road accidents

Did you know that road accidents are responsible for more deaths and injuries to travellers than anything else? If travelling by coach, travel with a well-established local firm if possible. Sitting near an exit is a good idea too. If you are driving whilst on holiday, as always, do not drink and drive. If you are hiring a car, ensure the tyres are in good condition and that there is a spare. Also, ensure the seat belts are working. Remember to find out who to contact if there is an accident or a problem.

Infected water

Visibly dirty water will be infective and should be avoided. Also, if someone is swimming at the bottom of a dirty pool, if they get into difficulties, it will not be noticeable.

Hazardous sports

Ensure that protective lifejackets are used whilst enjoying any water sports. Don't forget that you may require additional insurance if you are taking part in any risky sporting activity.

Alcohol and drugs

It is easy to drink more alcohol in a hot climate. Remember that local drinks can have a much higher alcohol content. Remember, do not drink alcohol when in charge of children.

Drowning

No one wants to think about drowning risks when going on holiday but unfortunately, this is a high-risk accident whilst away. It is essential that you observe your children at all times, never fall asleep at the poolside and avoid alcohol which will give you a false feeling of safety.

If someone has drowned:

- Start resuscitation measures immediately, if you can, start as you are pulling them out of the water. Even if there are no signs of life, resuscitation can be very successful.

- The cold water slows down the metabolic rate which leads to prolonged survival, especially in children, so do not give up resuscitating. Continue to resuscitate for up to 45 minutes.

- Once the casualty begins to breathe again, place them in the recovery position.

Effective travel insurance and the EHIC explained

You should ensure that you have effective travel insurance for all the family, but did you know that if you are travelling to the European Economic Area countries, you are entitled to apply for 'The European Health Insurance Card (EHIC)'? Since 2006, this has replaced the E111. The EHIC entitles you and your family to low cost or free state healthcare and covers you for treatment of pre-existing conditions too. You can also get free routine maternity care. More information can be found online at www.ehic.org.uk.

Fitness to travel

If you are flying to your holiday destination, there are important health issues to consider.

- If you or your child breaks a bone before holiday and you are flying, then you need to let whoever makes the cast know that you are flying and when. They can make a cast that will allow for any in-flight swelling.

- If major surgery to the abdomen has been performed, there needs to be at least two weeks allowed before flight.

- A four-week interval is required for any recent chest surgery. Also recent eye surgery poses a risk.

- Recent colds and nasal congestion can cause pressure behind the ear during flight so if any of you have had a recent cough, cold or ear pain, use steam inhalation to ease congestion.

- In the presence of severe earache, see your doctor and let them know that you intend to fly and when.

If you are at all concerned about fitness to fly issues, book an appointment with your usual doctor.

Flying

How can I ensure comfort during our flight?

- Cabin pressures can increase dehydration, causing headaches, dry throats, nasal congestion and increase the risk of a deep veined thrombosis in those at risk. Ensure that you all drink plenty of fluids such as water and uncarbonated drinks. Avoid alcohol, tea and coffee as they have a dehydrating effect.

- Wear loose, lightweight clothing.

- Carry your usual medicines in your hand luggage.

- Have spare socks and jumpers/cardigans in your hand luggage. The air-conditioning in flight can make you feel quite cold.

- Wear layers of clothing.

- Avoid wearing contact lenses during your flight as they can dry out.

- Get up and move around at intervals to help improve your circulation. This helps reduce swollen ankles and reduces the risk of deep veined thrombosis.

Motion sickness

This mostly affects children and can cause symptoms of feeling sick, dizzy, sweating and disorientation. Take travel sickness medicine at least one hour before flying, more details can be found in chapter 11. Another measure to prevent motion sickness is to nibble dry biscuits or crackers during the journey. If possible face the direction in which you are travelling, avoid reading and try to stay still. Sleeping may help. Some say that acupressure bands worn at the wrists are effective.

What is jet lag and how can I reduce the effects?

Jet lag is a collection of unpleasant symptoms which can occur if you have crossed five or more time zones, for example, five hours of flying or more. The symptoms can include, headache, exhaustion, insomnia, disorientation, poor concentration, appetite loss, dizziness, bowel and stomach disturbance. In some cases it can take up to a week to recover.

To minimise the effects of jet lag:

■ Take naps during your flight but avoid using sedation.

■ Increase your fluid intake as mentioned above. Avoid alcohol. Avoid sunbathing before your return flight home.

■ Take frequent walks around the cabin.

■ You could consider breaking a very long-haul flight with a stopover.

Medicines on-the-go and what to pack

It is always best to plan ahead. Think carefully about taking medicines with you on your holiday. Your practice nurse at your surgery will be able to help. Although many medicines can be bought over the counter in many developed countries, you cannot be sure of their authenticity.

Remember to keep medicines in a locked, airtight container, away from harm; particularly important if you have small children.

Always read the patient information leaflet carefully and discuss any concerns with your doctor, nurse or pharmacist. Never give more than the recommended daily dose.

Remember also to only use drugs if they are necessary. The human body has excellent immunity and often will heal itself. If you're unsure, always seek advice.

'The commonest drugs to be fake medicines (counterfeited) are antibiotics, anti-malarials, and anti-tuberculosis drugs. However, as these fakes are as likely to be doled out by doctors as by street-corner vendors, the only way to be sure of avoiding them is to buy your medicines from reputable sources in your home country. If you do need to take medicines prescribed abroad, ask about their origin.' Dr Nick Jones, author of *Travel Health – Planning Your Trip Worldwide – A Rough Guide*.

Listed below are some suggested medicines that are useful when on holiday. The drugs will be discussed in much more detail in chapter 11.

- Motion sickness tablets – Such as Joy-Rides or Sea-Legs.

- Painkillers – Such as paracetamol and ibuprofen.

- Antibiotics – These are only available in the UK on prescription. Your doctor or nurse is unlikely to prescribe these for you and your family on a just-in-case basis. Worldwide, antibiotics are overused, often treating viruses inappropriately. Overuse of antibiotics has lead to antibiotic resistance. If you feel an antibiotic is necessary, you need to seek medical advice first. It is important that you do not take leftover antibiotics with you or administer them. Inappropriate use can cause side effects and mask severe underlying disease. Always seek medical advice. If you or your family are prescribed antibiotics, always finish the course. This helps to reduce antibiotic resistance for all.

- Antihistamines – These drugs have multiple uses. You can buy these over the counter in the UK. They work by suppressing an allergic response to insect bites, hay fever, skin rashes, itching skin, even motion sickness. Again, side effects can occur, mainly drowsiness, although you can purchase non-drowsy antihistamines containing cetirizine hydrochloride or supermarket own brands which are normally just effective and a lot less costly.

- Laxatives – Changes in diet, fluid intake and routine can all contribute to changes in bowel function. To treat constipation, increase fluid intake and offer foods high in fibre such as dried prunes, figs, bran and spinach; but if all else fails, over-the-counter laxatives are very effective. Drugs such as senna or lactulose are very effective at restoring normal bowel function.

- Antidiarrhoeals – Diarrhoea is a common tummy upset that can affect the whole family. More worryingly, it can lead to dehydration, and prevention is even more important for the very young and the elderly. Please see chapter 6 for more details on dehydration. Rehydration sachets such as Dioralyte can be purchased over the counter. They help rehydration and replace any lost essential body salts.

- Anti-malarials – It is essential that you see your practice nurse for advice before travelling as you may or may not need these, depending on your destination. As mentioned, there are different ones on the market treating different types of malaria. The anti-malarials and duration of treatment vary, depending on your destination too. Some need to be purchased over the counter but others are prescribed on a private prescription which is only available from your surgery. Anti-malarials are not 100% effective, so it is important that you use an effective insect repellent which can be bought over the counter. Your practice nurse will be able to advise you fully.

- Insect repellents – DEET is known to be one of the most effective forms of insect repellent with virtually no side effects, although it can cause skin irritation. DEET can be found in the form of a spray. Remember to always follow the patient information leaflet sold with the treatment.

- Sun creams – If you are travelling to a hot country it is essential to use sun creams or sun blocks. As always, use a high factor, especially for young babies and small children. Try and purchase waterproof sun creams. Your pharmacist will be able to offer you good advice.

- Antiseptic creams and lotions – These are effective in treating cuts and grazes.

- Steroid creams – These are very effective for the treatment of eczema which can flare up due to new environmental triggers. They can also be effective in treating sunburn.

Pre-existing conditions

Order all your usual prescribed medicines well in advance. Many surgeries require at least 48 hours to issue prescription repeats and requests. If any of you have asthma, ensure that you have plenty of your usual inhalers, plus more than usual bronchodilator medicine, (relievers). Often asthma can become unstable in a foreign environment.

If you or your children have diabetes, you should stick to your usual injection and meal regimes. Always ensure that you have sugary drinks or sweets to reverse a possible hypo attack. Also, make sure that you have a letter from your doctor explaining why you have injections and blood glucose monitoring equipment with you. You can carry your insulin in your hand luggage in a cool bag to protect it but always check with your airline first.

It is helpful to have a letter regarding any existing conditions, written in the language of the country you are visiting.

You can access loads of helpful information at www.fitfortravel.nhs.uk. The general public and health professionals can use this site for free.

An app has been created for Android phones and the iPhone, which is free of charge. It is especially useful in emergencies. All you have to do is speak into the phone, the app will translate the words into one of 15 languages and then speak the message back. The app will also translate text in up to 57 languages. This is an excellent resource for travelling abroad.

'It is helpful to have a letter regarding any existing conditions, written in the language of the country you are visiting.'

Summing Up

- Your tour operator may not encourage travel vaccines even if they are required. Play it safe and visit your practice nurse where she can assess the needs of you and your family.

- It is important to protect against malaria if you are travelling to a high-risk country. Your practice nurse will be able to advise you. Remember to use insect repellents too.

- Take great care with food and water. Always eat food which is freshly cooked and use bottled water for drinking and brushing teeth.

- Protect your family from sunburn. Remember it is more risky between the hours of 10am and 3pm. Always use a high-factor sun cream, particularly for babies and small children and apply regularly.

- Accidents can occur around the pool – particularly drowning. Observe your children at all times.

- Make sure you and your family have adequate up-to-date travel health insurance.

- Painkillers, antidiarrhoeals and insect repellent are just some of the recommended useful medications to take on your travels.

- Always ensure you are prepared for travel with any necessary prescription medication used to treat pre-existing conditions.

Chapter Ten

Help From the Professionals

With the variety of healthcare practitioners working as part of the primary healthcare team, it can be very confusing deciding who to contact for help and advice.

If you need advice on any health-related matter, phone your surgery, where the receptionist should be only too happy to help. The more information that you can give your receptionist, the better she is able to help in offering you an appointment with the most suitable clinician. Please remember, they aren't being nosy or awkward, but they are trying the best that they can to offer you an appropriate appointment or advice.

This chapter focuses on the roles of the various healthcare professionals that you may encounter. Each section will explain briefly the differing roles of each clinician.

Your general practitioner (GP)

Specific role

A GP is a fully qualified doctor who is specialised as a GP working either at a surgery or health centre.

The main role of the GP is to diagnose, treat and refer patients to other agencies or specialities if required. They will have a broad range of knowledge. Your GP will be either a GP partner, or a salaried doctor, employed by a private

'The main role of the GP is to diagnose, treat and refer patients to other agencies or specialities if required. They will have a broad range of knowledge.'

medical practice or the NHS. You may come into contact with a locum GP. A locum doctor is able to work at differing practices and is hired on a session basis.

Your doctor will have a team of clinicians working alongside him or her, commonly including practice nurses, possibly a nurse practitioner, district nurses, health visitors, dieticians, midwives and school nurses.

Skills related to the role of GP

'Often your GP will have a special interest in areas such as chronic disease management, child health and child surveillance, minor surgical procedures or family planning.'

- Extensive knowledge and examination skills related to all systems of the body.

- Forms a diagnosis based on a range of symptoms and history taking, confirmed through excellent examination skills.

- Prescribes medicines and offers advice related to disease and long-term conditions.

- Refers patients for tests and investigations.

- Refers patient to a specialist if required.

- Often your GP will have a special interest in areas such as chronic disease management, child health and child surveillance, minor surgical procedures or family planning.

- Provides mental health services.

- Writes sick notes.

Your practice nurse

Specific role

Usually female, your practice nurse is a fully trained nurse who is employed either privately by your GP or by the NHS, working at your surgery or health centre. Your practice nurse works within the primary healthcare team. She will come into close contact with the same clinicians as the GP.

Some practice nurses have studied a degree level programme, giving them legal rights as a non-medical prescriber, entitling them to prescribe treatments related to their area of expertise.

Skills related to the role of practice nursing

- Running childhood immunisation clinics and travel clinics.
- Providing dressings and general treatment room duties.
- Offering a smoking cessation service.
- Offering lifestyle advice related to exercise and nutrition issues.
- Some offer family planning services.
- Women's health, coil checks and cervical smear tests.
- Health screening for prevention of illness and disease.
- Running chronic disease clinics related to asthma, heart disease, diabetes and kidney disease.

Your nurse practitioner

Specific role

A nurse practitioner is a qualified nurse who has had further training at degree level enabling them to provide care for a wide range of minor and more complex illnesses which would historically have been dealt with by a GP. Nurse practitioners have a wide range of assessment, history taking and clinical skills related to all the systems of the body, including ear, nose and throat conditions, chest and respiratory problems, skin, urinary and abdominal symptoms. Usually, your nurse practitioner will be legally entitled to prescribe a range of treatments within their area of expertise, having completed a programme of study. The extended role of the nurse practitioner offers rapid access to healthcare, working alongside and supporting the GP in providing appropriate care and an excellent, cost-effective service to patients.

'A nurse practitioner is a qualified nurse who has had further training at degree level enabling them to provide care for a wide range of minor and more complex illnesses which would historically have been dealt with by a GP.'

Skills related to the role of nurse practitioner

- History taking, examination and clinical skills to form a diagnosis.
- Able to diagnose and treat a wide range of conditions effectively.
- Can refer patients for specialist advice.
- Orders tests and investigations.
- Prescribes for a wide range of treatments, within her range of expertise.
- Offers health education and advice on lifestyle, diet and exercise.
- Refers more complex conditions to the GP.
- Provides extensive chronic disease advice and management.

Your health visitor

Specific role

'The health visitor is primarily involved with families with young children under the age of five but they also provide care for the elderly population.'

A health visitor will usually be a qualified registered general nurse, midwife or psychiatric nurse who has gained specialist skills and qualifications in community health, child health, health promotion and health education.

The health visitor is primarily involved with families with young children under the age of five but they also provide care for the elderly population. The health visitor will also offer advice and support to pregnant women. She will normally focus on delivering advice on a range of topics related to staying healthy and avoiding illness.

The health visitor works closely with your GP, school nurses, speech therapists, social services and your practice nurse. You can find out who your health visitor is by contacting your surgery where they will be happy to offer contact information.

Skills related to the role of health visitor

- Advises on child growth and development.

- Advises on prevention of common illnesses and infections.

- Offers breastfeeding, weaning and teething advice.

- Offers behavioural advice on issues such as potty training, play and interaction with others.

- Advises on healthy eating, hygiene matters, exercise and safety in the home.

- Supports vulnerable families, in particular with postnatal depression, bereavement or violence in the home.

- Runs baby clinics where you can get baby weighed and meet other mums.

Your community midwife

Specific role

Your community midwife will have had either direct entry into midwifery training, or following registration as a general registered nurse. She will have specialist skills related to all aspects of pregnancy and childbirth and will take care of all the expectant mother's needs, so long as there are no complications, in which case, she will refer the mother to the medical team.

A midwife works in partnership with a team of midwives, the GP, practice nurse and health visitor.

Skills related to the role of community midwife

- Provides antinatal care either at home or in a clinic situation.

- Offers health education and lifestyle advice such as diet and exercise, relating to pregnancy.

- Prepares mothers for parenthood.

- Offers advice on home or hospital birth.

- Assists and support mother during labour.

- Offers breastfeeding and bottle feeding advice.

- Provides care for newborn babies up to four weeks post delivery.
- Offers postnatal care for the new mother.

Your school nurse

Specific role

The school nurse is usually from a general nurse background having completed a degree such as 'Specialist practitioner – School nurse/Specialist community Public Health Nurse'.

If your child is of school age, you can contact her through the school if you have any concerns.

The school nurse works closely with the wider healthcare team, including your GP, the health visitors and practice nurse.

Skills related to the role of school nurse

- Provides health and sex education to schools.
- Runs and provides immunisation programmes to school-aged children.
- Monitors child health and development.
- Deals with child protection issues and mental health issues.
- Offers advice regarding bullying.
- Offers lifestyle advice including dietary and exercise advice.
- Provides a wide range of health promotion advice.

Your local pharmacist

Specific role

Pharmacists graduate from university with extensive knowledge regarding all medicines. Working in street pharmacies, health centres and shopping centres, and working to strict legal and ethical guidelines, pharmacists deal with controlling, dispensing and distributing medicines and drugs.

Currently, they are already dealing with people of all ages with minor ailments. It is reassuring to know that your local pharmacist will have the skills to decide if he or she can help or if you need more expert advice from a nurse practitioner or your GP.

The government is currently running a scheme which promotes more widely the use of pharmacists in their role of managing minor ailments. They can also prescribe many prescription-only medicines.

Skills related to the role of pharmacist

- Assesses if you need referral to your GP for further advice.
- Dispenses drugs and medicines as prescribed by a designated clinician.
- Provides advice related to taking medicines including side effects and interactions with other drugs.
- Arranges delivery of prescriptions to some patients.
- Sells over-the-counter medicines, advising how to use safely and effectively.
- Undertakes 'medicine use reviews'.
- Counsels and treats minor ailments.
- Provides smoking cessation services.
- Offers health checks, such as blood pressure monitoring and obesity management.
- Offers family planning related to the emergency contraceptive pill.

- Keeps a register of controlled drugs.
- Manages a needle and syringe exchange service.

Summing Up

- There is a whole team of clinicians available; all dedicated to providing care and advice for the needs of you and your family.

- Your GP will normally work at your surgery or local health centre. He or she mainly deals with illness and disease, offering treatment and support. Many GPs have a special interest including areas such as family planning, minor surgery and child health.

- Practice nurses mainly deal with health promotion and management of chronic diseases such as diabetes and asthma. They also provide general treatment room services.

- Nurse practitioners work alongside and support GPs. They can offer same-day appointments and can diagnose and treat both complex and minor ailments and diseases. They can usually prescribe medicines.

- Health visitors mostly care for children under the age of five and the elderly population. They are involved in child protection and offer support for families with special needs. They are very much involved in childhood development.

- Midwives offer support during pregnancy and for the first four weeks following delivery. They prepare mothers for parenthood and offer lifestyle support. They also give breastfeeding advice and assist mothers during delivery.

- School nurses care for children over five. They are also involved in childhood development and offer sex education to schools. They deal with bullying issues and health promotion.

- Pharmacists offer a range of services from advice on managing minor ailments, through to routine health checks for obesity. They dispense the medication prescribed by the designated clinician and offer advice on side effects.

Chapter Eleven

Your Home Medicine Chest

'Nearly 9 out of every 10 people often treat minor ailments themselves – 42% do it all the time and 95% say they are confident in treating their own minor ailments without seeing a doctor'. *OTC Directory 2008/2009 Treatments for Common Ailments*.

In this chapter, we shall look at common medicines that would be useful to have in your medicine chest. There are hundreds of medicines that you can purchase over the counter and listing all of these goes beyond the scope of this book, but we have endeavoured to list those most commonly used at home. Visiting your pharmacist for advice will allow them to suggest any specific treatments which you may need.

Pharmacists are fully trained in medicines and managing minor illnesses. In terms of minor illnesses, they can often assist you in caring for your child and family, without the need for an appointment with your GP.

When buying a medicine for your child, you will need to tell the pharmacist your child's age, what the main symptoms are, if your child has any drug allergies, what treatment has already been used, and if your child is on any other current medicine. Also remember to tell them if your child has any health conditions such as asthma.

What are the differences between 'over-the-counter medicines' (OTC) and 'prescription-only medicines' (POM)?

- OTCs are any medicine which you can purchase from a pharmacy or store which do not require a prescription. Some of these drugs, such as Calpol and Nurofen, can be prescribed also. The difference is that prescriptions issued for a child under the age of 18 will be free of charge, whereas drugs over the counter incur a charge.

- POMs are only available on prescription, written by a fully trained health professional who is legally entitled to issue the prescription. Historically, only doctors were able to prescribe. However, today, dentists, nurses and pharmacists are able to prescribe if they have undertaken a period of extensive study at university, enabling them to prescribe effectively, safely, appropriately and cost-effectively.

Making the most of your medicines

- It is always important to keep all medicines out of reach of small children. Also, ensure that they are kept in a cool, dark place.

- Remember to regularly check the expiry date, which will be written somewhere on the outer packaging. Any out-of-date drugs should be given back to your local pharmacist. Never put them in the bin or down the toilet.

- Keep all medicines in their original boxes or containers. Unnecessary handling of medicines can alter the chemical balance.

- Always read the label and check the dose is appropriate and only give the recommended dose.

- Remember to read your patient information leaflet where you will be advised how to take your medicine and what likely side effects may occur.

Recommended medicines to keep at home

Medicines for pain and fever

- Children's paracetamol (Calpol) – Can be given from the age of 3 months for the treatment of pain and fever. It is very effective but must be taken carefully and never give more than the recommended dose. Paracetamol is effective for mild to moderate pain, especially effective against earache, teething, aches and pains associated with colds and flu, and sore throats. It can be given four times within 24 hours but always ensure at least four hours lapse between doses.

  Paracetamol is often used for post-vaccination fever and pain. It should not be used for those with known fructose intolerance and used with caution in kidney disease or liver disease. Adverse reactions are rare.

- Children's ibuprofen (Nurofen) – Can be used from the age of three months. Used for fast, effective relief for mild to moderate pain, inflammatory pain and swelling. It can be administered every 6-8 hours, with a maximum three doses in 24 hours. It should not be used in anyone who has previously had a reaction to it as it can cause asthma, rhinitis, urticaria (an allergy rash which looks like nettle rash). Again, it should be used with caution in those with liver or kidney disease. It should not be taken if your child is receiving oral steroids for treatment of an asthma attack. The two drugs used together are dangerous. Side effects are unusual but can include rashes and urticaria. If this happens, stop the treatment.

'Paracetamol is effective for mild to moderate pain, especially effective against earache, teething, aches and pains associated with colds and flu, and sore throats.'

Skin emollients and barrier creams

- Doublebase cream – This is a long-lasting, hydrating and moisturising barrier cream, used to treat dry and itchy skin conditions. It can be used as often as you desire and drug reactions are rare. It is also available as a shower gel and bath additive.

- E45 – This is an emollient used for the treatment of dry, flaking, itching skin conditions such as eczema. It can also be used to treat sunburn. You can use it two to three times daily and side effects are rare.

- Hydromol cream – This is another effective treatment to sooth dermatitis, dry skin and eczema. It is particularly effective if applied after a bath or shower, when the skin is warm. Side effects are rare.

> Apply all creams and lotions in gentle strokes in the direction that the hair is growing. This helps prevent inflammation around the hair follicles. Also, do not rub in vigorously, as this causes inflammation.

Nappy rash treatments

- Drapolene cream – You should wash and dry the skin first and then apply, paying particular attention to the skin folds. Drapolene can also be used effectively for sunburn and minor burns. Side effects are rare.

- Morhulin ointment – This is another very effective treatment for nappy rash. It can be applied directly to the skin, up to three times daily. Side effects are also rare. Morhulin can also be used for the treatment of minor wounds, cuts and eczema.

Warts and verruca treatment

- Bazuka gel – A topical treatment for removal of warts, verrucas, corns and calluses. It should be used each night after soaking the affected area in warm water for two to three minutes. Then dry thoroughly. Apply one to two drops of the gel to the affected area and allow to dry. Try and avoid the surrounding healthy skin. Once weekly, use an emery board or pumice stone on the lesion. Treatment may be necessary for several weeks before the lesion resolves.

- Salactol wart paint – This is another popular treatment for warts and verrucas. It should be used at night also. Wash the affected area in warm water, dry the skin and apply a few drops to the lesion, carefully allowing each drop to dry before applying another. Also, cover the wart with a plaster for 24 hours, until the next treatment is required.

Headlice and parasite treatments

- Derbac M – This is used to eradicate headlice and scabies. It should be applied to the affected area and allowed to dry. Leave for twelve hours before washing off. Following this, use a nit comb to remove all dead lice. It should not be used on babies under the age of six months.

- Lyclear – This can also be used for the effective removal of headlice. It should be used after first washing and towel-drying the hair. Apply to the hair and scalp, giving particular attention to behind the ears and the nape of the neck. Leave on for ten minutes and then wash thoroughly and dry in the usual way.

- Mebendazole oral suspension – This is used for the treatment of a number of types of worms, particularly threadworms. It is safe for children over two years up to adults. If you suspect re-infection, treat again in two weeks.

- Pripsen tablets – These are used for the treatment of threadworms only. They are safe to use from the age of two. Again, if re-infection is suspected, treat again two weeks later.

Cradle cap treatment

- Dentinox cradle cap treatment shampoo – Use two applications at each bath time. Massage into wet hair, rinse and repeat. Then rinse fully and dry as usual.

- Metanium cradle cap cream – When treating infants over the age of twelve months, you should massage carefully into the affected area. Leave on for between thirty minutes and two hours, depending on the severity of the affected area and then wash and dry. For infants under twelve months, you should only leave on for a maximum thirty minutes and then wash off and dry. If a second treatment is needed, then wait seven days.

Travel sickness tablets

- Joy-Rides – It is raspberry flavoured chewable tablet and can be taken any time during the journey but it is more effective if taken twenty minutes before travelling. There are mild side effects sometimes, mainly dry mouth and possible dizziness.

- Sea-Legs – Sea-Legs can be given to children over the age of two years for the prevention and treatment of motion sickness or travel sickness. It is best given one hour before travel but can be given the night before too.

Medicines for allergy, hay fever and bites

- Clarityn allergy syrup – This is an effective antihistamine for the treatment of allergic rhinitis (hay fever) and urticaria (hives). Given as a once daily dose, it is very effective with minimal side effects. It cannot be used for children under the age of two. It should be used with caution with those with liver disease or glaucoma.

- Piriton – This is used for the treatment of hay fever, rhinitis, urticaria, food allergies and insect bites. It can be used in children over the age of one. Common side effects include drowsiness, sedation, blurred vision, nausea and a dry mouth. It should be used with caution with anyone with epilepsy or glaucoma.

- Flixonase allergy nasal spray – This is an effective anti-inflammatory used for the treatment of hay fever and rhinitis. It can be used from the age of four. There is a delayed onset of action, whereby relief of symptoms may take a number of days to be noticed. Common side effects include headache, nasal and throat dryness or irritation.

- Beconase nasal spray – This is an anti-inflammatory spray used for the treatment of allergic rhinitis (hay fever). It is licensed for use over the age of six. Common side effects include a rash, an unpleasant taste or smell, nose bleeds and throat or nasal dryness.

- Eurax cream – This is a very effective cream used for the treatment of itch in dry skin conditions including sunburn, eczema, allergic rashes, chickenpox, insect bites and stings, hives and nettle rash. It can be applied two to three times daily and offers relief for between six to ten hours.

Treatments for coughs and colds, catarrh and congestion

Cough and cold therapies are no longer licensed for children aged 0-6. There is not enough evidence available regarding safety issues when used in young children.

- Dark chocolate – Did you know it has a scientific value in treating coughs?

- Otrivine nasal drops – This can be used for those aged over six years for the treatment of nasal congestion and hay fever and sinusitis. Otrivine should be used twice a day in children aged six to twelve and three times daily from the age of thirteen. For children you should only treat for five days and for adults treat for seven. If you treat beyond this time, once you stop treatment, you can get rebound symptoms. Mild side effects include a dry mouth. It shouldn't be used on anyone using medication to treat high blood pressure.

- Non-drowsy Sudafed children's syrup – Used four times daily for a maximum of five days, this is effective in reducing congestion and relieving coughs. It is not licensed for children under the age of six. Common side effects include irritability, sleep disturbances, nausea and vomiting and possibly headache. This medicine should not be used on anyone using blood pressure tablets, anyone with an overactive thyroid, or severe kidney disease.

- Covonia vapour drops – An effective treatment for congestion, hay fever and catarrh from the age of three months. It contains menthol and peppermint oil. A few drops should be put on a handkerchief and inhaled. Do not allow to come into contact with the eyes.

'Cough and cold therapies are no longer licensed for children aged 0-6. There is not enough evidence available regarding safety issues when used in young children.'

Medicines for grazes, minor burns and scratches

- Savlon antiseptic cream – This is very effective in preventing and treating skin infections. Spread gently on the blister, burn or small wound to clean and protect. You can treat sunburn with it too.

- Germolene antiseptic cream – This effective cream prevents and treats minor skin infections whilst acting as a gentle local anaesthetic and barrier cream. Treats minor burns, scalds, blisters, stings and bites, and chapped and rough skin. Side effects are rare, but include a rash.

Medicines for teething

- Anbesol teething gel – Used four times daily, this soothing gel contains local anaesthetic and disinfectant for the treatment of teething, mouth ulcers and dental irritation.

- Bonjela teething gel – This is licensed for use only in children over the age of two months, for the treatment of teething pain. Bonjela contains antibacterial and anaesthetic properties. It can be used every three hours.

Medicines for colic, diarrhoea and constipation

- Dioralyte – This is an excellent rehydration treatment for diarrhoea. It comes in a number of flavours and is mixed with water, replacing the salts and minerals lost during diarrhoea. A child under the age of two with prolonged diarrhoea should always be seen by a doctor.

- Infacol – This can be used for griping pain and colic. Given before each feed, it can provide progressive improvement over a number of days. There have been no reported undesirable effects. It works by breaking down gas bubbles and makes them easier to pass.

- Gripe water – This is used for the relief of wind in infants under the age of one year and can be used up to six times in twenty-four hours.

- Syrup of figs – This is a safe and effective treatment to relieve occasional constipation. It should be used short term and can be used for babies over the age of one. There are no known side effects.

Summing Up

- Be wary of side effects and stop any medicines if you believe they are causing an adverse reaction. Always consult with your doctor or nurse practitioner if you or your child experience side effects. In doing so, they can advised you on an alternative and report the side effects to the drug company and MHRA (Medicines and Healthcare products Regulatory Agency) through the 'yellow card system'.

- Many pharmacists are now trained to diagnose and treat minor illnesses. Why not visit your local chemist where you can get advice and avoid the inconvenience of trying to book an appointment at your surgery.

- Always store medicines safely, in a locked cupboard, out of reach of children.

- Remember to check the expiry date of your medicine. Never use if out of date.

- Never discard unwanted medicines in the dustbin and never flush them down the toilet. Take them back to your pharmacy where they can be disposed of safely.

Glossary

Antibiotic resistance
This relates to how a bacteria is able to resist the effect of an antibiotic, therefore rendering the antibiotic ineffective against disease.

Cyanosis
Is a term used to describe the bluish tinge to the skin, ears, nose, fingers or lips as a result of a lack of oxygen in the blood.

Droplet infection
Is infection which is contracted through inhaling germs that are airborne.

Endemic disease
Relates to a natural disease which is particular to a given country or region.

Eradicate
In relation to disease, this means to completely eliminate a given disease.

Exacerbate
Means to intensify or worsen a disease or condition.

Faeces
Another word for poo or stool.

Immunological memory
Describes how the immune system has the ability to recognise and respond rapidly to an antigen.

Incubation period
Is the interval between exposure to infection and the onset of symptoms.

Mucus membrane
A membrane that lines all passages of the body such as the mouth, nose, ears and anus, which secretes protective mucus.

Paediatrician
A consultant doctor who specialises in child health and illness.

Paroxysm
A sudden violent attack.

Prophylactic treatment
Relates to medicines or treatment given to prevent a disease process.

Rebound symptoms
This occurs sometimes when a treatment is stopped suddenly. The original symptoms suddenly return.

Red flag
Is a term used that describes, for example, a sign or symptom indicating a medical emergency.

Stridor
Describes noisy breathing which is often high-pitched and can sometimes be a sign of obstruction.

Yellow card system
This is a system that prescribers use to report any unwanted side effects or adverse reactions to any drugs.

Help List

Active Press

www.activeplaces.org
This useful website lets you search for sports facilities anywhere in England.

Medicinechestonline

www.medicine-chest.co.uk
A directory of medicines and food supplements that are avaliable over the counter from your pharmacist.

Mentor

www.webmentorlibrary.com
The most comprehensive and widely used diagnostic decision support tool in the UK, used by more than 55% of GPs and health practitioners.

NHS Choices

www.eatwell.gov.uk
Offers advice on healthy diet and nutrition.
www.nhs.uk/livewell/Pharmacy/pages/Yourmedicinecabinet.aspx
Offers advice and suggestions on what medicines to keep at home.

Slimming World

www.slimmingworld.com/imformation/sitemap.aspx

Weight Watchers

www.weightwatchers.co.uk

Book List

ABC of Eyes Third Edition
Khaw P, Elkinton, AR, (1999) – BMJ Books

Caring for Kids- A Self-Care Guide to Childhood Ailments
Doctor Patient Partnership

Essentials of Pathophysiology
C, Porth. (2004) – Lippincott Williams & Wilkins

First Aid Manual – Revised 9th Edition
St John Ambulance, St Andrew's First Aid, British Red Cross, (2011) – Dorling Kindersley London

Fundamentals of Anatomy & Physiology Fifth Edition
F, Martini (2001) – Prentice Hall

Health Information for Overseas Travel 2001 Edition
DH Department of Health (2001) – The Stationary Office. London

Immunization: Childhood and Travel Health Fourth Edition
G. Kassianos (2001) – Blackwell Science

OTC Directory – Treatment For Common Ailments
Proprietary Association of Great Britain (2008/2009) – Vernon House London

Oxford Handbook of General Practice
C, Simon, H, Everitt, J, Birtwistle, B, Stevenson (2004) – Oxford Universtiy Press

Symptom Sorter
K, Hopcroft. V, Forte (1999) – Radcliffe Medical Press

Travel Health – Planning your Trip Worldwide – A Rough Guide
N, Jones (2004) – Special London

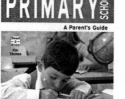